America's Sunset Coast

By Merrill Windsor
Photographed by James A. Sugar

Prepared by the Special Publications Division
National Geographic Society, Washington, D. C.

America's Sunset Coast

By Merrill Windsor

Photographed by James A. Sugar

Published by
The National Geographic Society
Robert E. Doyle, *President*
Melvin M. Payne, *Chairman of the Board*
Gilbert M. Grosvenor, *Editor*
Melville Bell Grosvenor, *Editor Emeritus*

Prepared by
The Special Publications Division
Robert L. Breeden, *Editor*
Donald J. Crump, *Associate Editor*
Philip B. Silcott, *Senior Editor*
Barbara Grazzini, *Senior Researcher
   and Assistant to the Editor*
Kathleen F. Teter, *Researcher*

Illustrations and Design
William L. Allen, *Picture Editor*
Jody Bolt, *Art Director*
Suez B. Kehl, *Assistant Art Director*
Cinda Rose, *Design Assistant*

Mary Ann Harrell, *Editor, Picture Legends*
   William L. Allen, Jody Bolt, Thomas Bolt,
   Linda McCarter Bridge, Jan Leslie Cook,
   Toni Eugene, Barbara Grazzini,
   Daniel E. Hutner, Suzanne Venino,
   Picture Legends

Map Research and Production
John D. Garst, Jr., Virginia L. Baza,
   Cathy Wells, Alfred L. Zebarth

Production and Printing
Robert W. Messer, *Production Manager*
George V. White, *Assistant Production Manager*
Raja D. Murshed, June L. Graham,
   Christine A. Roberts, David V. Showers,
   Production Assistants

Debra A. Antonini, Barbara Bricks,
   Jane H. Buxton, Rosamund Garner,
   Suzanne J. Jacobson, Amy E. Metcalfe,
   Cleo Petroff, Katheryn M. Slocum,
   Suzanne Venino, *Staff Assistants*
Brit Aabakken Peterson, *Index*

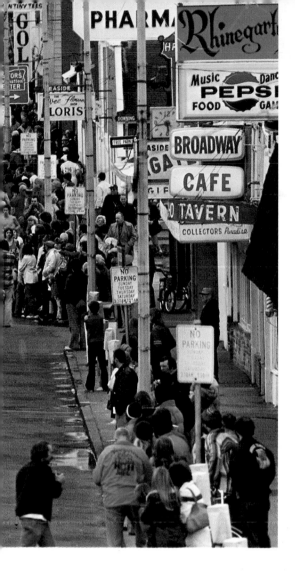

Contents

Surging waves of runners break
into the annual Trail's End Marathon.
The race winds 26 grueling miles through
town and countryside, returning to the start
at Seaside—a favorite Oregon resort.

PRECEDING PAGES: *After the last ride
of the day, surfers head homeward
as a flaming sun slips below the horizon
off Rincon Point in southern California
(pages 2-3). Coast redwoods reach skyward
on the northern California shore (page 1).
On a warm December evening, riders
splash along the beach where California
meets Mexico (front endpaper).*

Roaring wall of white water
crashes down upon a surfer
at Huntington Beach,
California, dooming his ride.
A temperate climate invites
southern Californians outdoors
the year round—but chill
Pacific waves often prompt
even the most determined
surfers and divers
to wear wet suits for warmth.

FOLLOWING PAGES:
Santa Monica, a suburb
of Los Angeles, faces the sea
from atop 100-foot-high bluffs.
Heavy winter rains have
temporarily discouraged
beachgoers, but in the summer
months sun worshipers wedge
together on the sand, and
fishermen jam the pier.
An offshore breakwater, built
in 1950, provides a sheltering
anchorage for pleasure boats.

Twilight settles around seals straggling ashore to their rookery on San Miguel

island in the Santa Barbara Channel. At night, they huddle in groups on the beach.

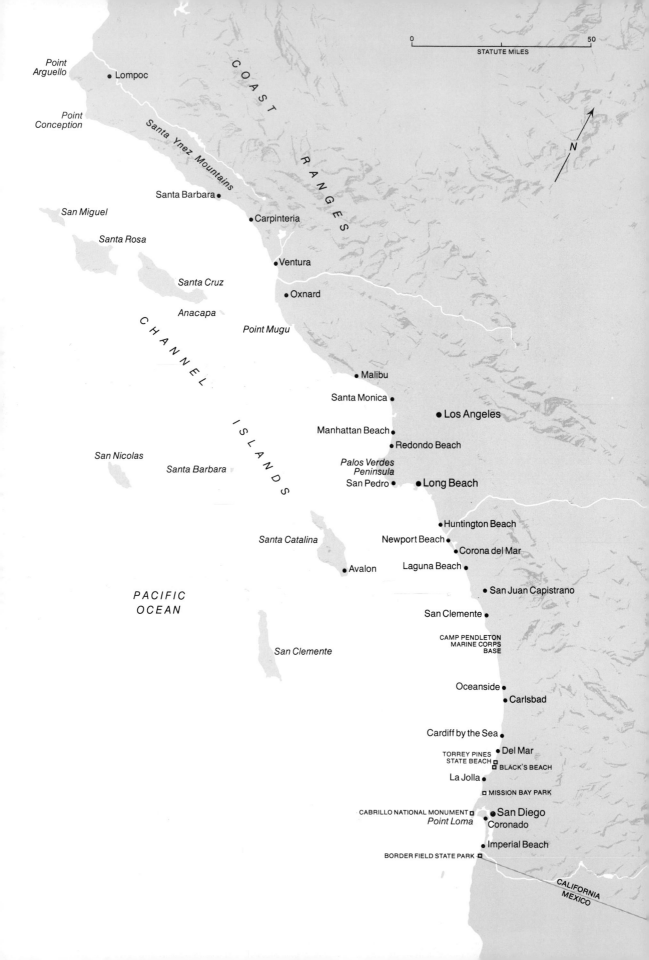

Part I: Southern California

AS IF LOST IN PRIVATE MEMORIES, the stone figure looks down from Point Loma toward a sheltered inlet where the United States Navy berths its submarines. The sculpture is the likeness of Juan Rodríguez Cabrillo, a 16th-century Portuguese explorer in the service of Spain. It occupies the place of honor at Cabrillo National Monument above San Diego Harbor.

My eyes followed the statue's gaze to the water's edge, and I thought: This is where it all began—the series of events that converted a remote wilderness into one of the most visited, most chronicled, and, in places, most populated and industrialized coastal strips in the world.

And yet, even now—more than four centuries after Captain Cabrillo led his men ashore at Ballast Point—America's Sunset Coast is only partially transformed. Perhaps it is most intriguing because of the recurring contrast it offers between nature's handiwork and man's intrusion. The sequence of beaches and bluffs, headlands and bays, cities and harbors, farms and forests that reaches from the Mexican border 1,293 miles north to Washington's rock-walled Cape Flattery is as richly varied as any shoreline anywhere. Both man and nature have contributed to that variety, as they have to the coast's beauty and its deterioration. They form an uneasy partnership, for neither can fully trust the other.

This book explores a long, slender ribbon of land and water, and presents a sampling of the people who live, work, and play there. It is not the story of the West Coast as a region, of the Pacific states and their great cities. Rather it is tightly limited to the very western edge of California, Oregon, and Washington. Photographer Jim Sugar and I tried never to travel more than five miles from the ocean in pursuit of a subject. Sometimes we detoured a bit farther out to sea; the Channel Islands, after all, are part of the coastal zone. But mostly we were close to sand and surf.

The coastline we traversed was formed by classic geologic forces: wind and water and the convulsive folding and faulting of the earth itself. But the dominant agent is the sea. Alternately invading and retreating, it has left behind great layers of sedimentary rock built upon the continent's granite foundation. Elsewhere it has submerged the land; many bays and estuaries

Lure of its rare combination of climate, scenery, and natural resources has made southern California the most populous part of the Pacific Coast. Harbors, resorts, and residential communities merge along a shoreline of white crescent beaches and rocky cliffs. Offshore, the Channel Islands—the tops of submerged mountains—rise above the surf to provide havens for marine wildlife.

are drowned rivers or fault valleys. The sea works from minute to minute as well as from age to age. Armed with waves, tides, and currents, it constantly assaults the land. It shapes dramatic promontories and inlets. Polishing a worn-down terrace, it forms a long, broad beach. In a single, raging storm, it may wash the sand from a sloping strand and leave instead a shelf of pebbles, cobbles, and shells.

In these pages we hope to convey some sense of the wealth of variety along this remarkable coast—in terms both of physical geography and of living things, and particularly of human activity. And that brings us back to Juan Rodríguez Cabrillo.

IN 1542, CABRILLO and the crews of his two small ships, the *San Salvador* and the *Victoria*, lingered less than a week at San Diego, or the Bay of San Miguel as they called it. They arrived on September 28, repaired their equipment, took aboard fresh water, and sailed away on October 3. They were the first Europeans to touch foot on the western shore of what is now the United States. Cabrillo died three months later, but his comrades continued northward, perhaps as far as Oregon, before returning to Mexico.

Yet their brave venture caused little stir among the officials of New Spain—since they found neither treasure nor the fabled sea passage across North America—and further exploration of the coast was only sporadic. More than two centuries passed before the soldier Don Gaspar de Portolá and the mission-building priest Junípero Serra arrived at San Diego to begin the slow and difficult task of colonization.

Hostile conditions and bad fortune were the enemy, not the native population. Unlike such fierce tribes as the Apaches and the Sioux in other parts of the West, California's coastal Indians offered little resistance. Instead, the newcomers were plagued by illness and injury, chronic shortages of food and equipment, internal disagreements, and indifference in Mexico City.

Nevertheless, Serra and his colleagues persevered. In time the chain of Franciscan missions grew to 21, with productive fields, orchards, and pastures that became the foundation of the great ranchos when Mexico freed herself from Spain and then secularized church lands.

California remained essentially pastoral until the middle of the 19th century. When the discovery of gold in the north created a city called San Francisco almost overnight, Los Angeles was still a drowsy village. Its own dramatic growth awaited transcontinental rail service. But by the early 1900's, southern California was not only a major agricultural empire but also a locale for such exotic new industries as motion pictures and aviation.

Today, the southern part of the Pacific coastline is by far the most heavily populated. Here a mild climate and the gentle terrain of coastal basins and river valleys have combined to encourage almost solid urban development. Southern California's two major cities, Los Angeles and San Diego, are both on the coast; so are dozens of smaller communities from Imperial Beach to Santa Barbara. Indeed, the fringes of the Los Angeles and San Diego metropolitan areas would likely have merged by now, except for a huge military preserve that separates them like a carefully placed buffer. The Marine Corps' Camp Pendleton includes the last large piece of southern California coastal land left in its natural state.

This coast owes its favorable climate not only to its southerly latitudes, and its location away from the main path of Pacific storms, but also to its orientation. From San Diego to Point Conception, the coastline curves northwest to west, shielded on the north by mountains. Prevailing westerly winds and moderating ocean currents help maintain comfortable temperatures

*Warmest, driest climate of the Sunset Coast prevails
in its southernmost section. From the Mexican border
to Point Conception (area defined by rectangle),
the coastline curves northwest, protected on the north
by mountain ranges. Along the beaches, summer ocean
temperatures may warm to the low 70's. Dry San Diego
—its mean annual rainfall measures ten inches—has
a year-round temperature pattern so uniform that summer
maximums average only 75° F., winter minimums 48.*

most of the time, regardless of season. Moreover, the winds generally keep the coastline free of the smog that plagues so many of the inland valleys of southern California. San Diego is known for an especially equable climate.

WHEN I HAD ARRIVED at Point Loma, visibility was limited to perhaps a mile. But now a bright sun was burning off the morning fog, and when I looked southeast from the visitor center I could see the hills of Baja California beyond the Mexican border. My eyes traced the Pacific shoreline northward along the peninsula whose slender Silver Strand encloses the southern extension of San Diego Bay. Toward its northern end the land widens and turns deep green with the lawns and trees of Coronado, then gray with the concrete of North Island Naval Air Station.

To east and north spread the panorama of San Diego, city and harbor, enhanced by the gracefully curved coronet of the Coronado Bridge. As I watched, a procession of aircraft approached and took off from the air station and Lindbergh Field, San Diego's international airport. Boats and ships plied the harbor channels.

The heights of Point Loma masked the view to the northwest, but my memory carried much farther than I could have seen anyway. Beyond the ridgeline lies the land-and-water interplay of Mission Bay Park. North of La Jolla's palm-lined beaches rise the cliffs of Torrey Pines mesa, home of a rare species of pine tree.

When the sloping beaches resume, they prevail for nearly a hundred miles, broken here and there by bluffs or rocky eruptions or the marinas of the Orange County coast. Then comes the east-west arc of Long Beach, ending at the harbor-industrial complex of Terminal Island and San Pedro and the jutting shoulders of the Palos Verdes Peninsula.

North of the peninsula the broad beaches begin again, and the place-names sound a familiar roll: Redondo Beach, Manhattan Beach, Santa Monica, Malibu. Near Oxnard and Ventura, citrus groves come almost to the water; at Santa Barbara the Santa Ynez Mountains rise abruptly just behind the city, capped by peaks that reach more than 4,000 feet high.

At Point Conception, the west-running shoreline turns toward the north, and the effects are immediately noticeable: colder temperatures in the water, more fog and chillier air on the land. Climatically and psychologically, coastal southern California ends at Point Conception.

"The surf plays its endless, rhythmic game"

AT FIVE O'CLOCK on a November morning the San Diego sky was black, and except for her tiny running lamps the fishing boat *Mary Ann* was dark as we moved through the harbor. Yet my main impression was not of the darkness, but rather of the soft gleam of lights that ringed the upper bay and reflected in long streaks on the water: lights of piers, streets, and buildings, of aircraft hangars and runways, of bridges and hills, their glow punctuated by the flash of airfield beacons and the blinking of channel buoys.

The *Mary Ann*'s diesel engine throbbed steadily. In the outer harbor Tony Giacalone increased our speed, and I moved forward on the narrow deck to catch the full effect of the fresh sea breeze. Out of sight in the gloom ahead was Joe DeSanti, Tony's partner, in *La Diana*—like *Mary Ann* a 32-foot cedar-hulled boat more than 40 years old and still sturdy and dependable.

The two men represent a declining number of commercial fishermen who employ the old-fashioned long-line method. Increased competition, the efficiency of nets, and the demands of a single-man boat have brought the change. But Tony and Joe stick with their vanishing art. Friends since boyhood, they almost always fish in sight of each other and combine their catch.

I watched the emerging mountain skyline to the east. A bank of gray clouds gradually turned vermilion, then lightened to gold. As we caught up with Joe's boat, half a dozen naval vessels loomed in the dawn light. A few minutes later the aircraft carrier *Constellation* passed within a hundred yards, towering over us like a seagoing skyscraper.

Another quarter hour and we had reached the day's fishing grounds. Tony started paying out his nylon lines from the round, flat baskets in which they were carefully coiled.

Hooks baited with silvery anchovies dangled at four-foot intervals. As he worked, tying one line to the next and throwing out oil-can buoys to support them, he used his hands, his teeth, sometimes an elbow. All the while, raucous sea gulls wheeled and flapped overhead, swooping down to try to steal bait before it could sink.

Soon Tony's lines lay connected in a narrow oval about a mile long. Later as we hauled in the catch, many of the hooks came up empty, but a fair number of them brought in glistening prizes, usually rock cod or sculpin.

Halfway through this chore the boats moved together, and I jumped aboard *La Diana*. Joe was pulling in a good many chunky, bright orange-red sculpin. "Gold (*Continued on page 33*)

New twist to an old sport: Rick Hoolko skims over San Diego's Mission Bay on a Windsurfer, a 12-foot-long board with a mast and a sail, but no rudder. To steer, he tilts the sail with a wishbone-shaped boom, leaning to balance the force of the wind. Just over a decade old, wind surfing has gained many enthusiasts here and abroad.

Winter reverie: Salt-sharpened breezes and bathing-suit temperatures bring a December day to its close for Kristy Souza (standing) and Jamie Martin—after a race on the smooth sands of Border Field State Park. Here, riders sometimes let their mounts go at full gallop for about a mile, almost to the Mexican border. "The weather is good most of the year," says Kristy, "and whenever it is, I go riding." On warm days she takes her horse out "to where he has to swim, a little beyond the breakers."

One more prize flashes onto the deck as Joe DeSanti hauls in a fishing line, five miles off San Diego aboard his 32-footer La Diana. Single-handed, relying on his own strength and skill, he pays out or brings in lines that, when attached end to end, form a mile-long oval in the sea. Each line holds some 500 hooks, baited with anchovies and set out to drift on leaders at four-foot intervals, then cleared of fish during the day's run. The heavy labor involved, along with the increased use of nets, has caused a decline in long-lining, which may earn $250 a day in good weather. DeSanti always fishes alone; his friend Tony Giacalone usually works nearby, in a similar sturdy cedar-hulled boat.

Helm in hand, octogenarian Vincenzo Giacalone pauses
while giving his grandsons an account of his time as
a crewman on the Star of India, a square-rigger preserved
at San Diego. He sailed on her San Francisco-Alaska
runs in 1914 and 1915. Later he brought a bride from
his native Sicily and became a fisherman, settling in
San Diego because "its climate was like home."

Lights *blaze in early evening in the Central Library at the University of California at San Diego, which houses 750,000 books and 30 special research collections. The eight-level concrete and glass structure, completed in 1970, rises above a eucalyptus grove at mid-campus. In the library's plaza, a martial-arts team performs a drill. Across campus in the university natatorium, a student demonstrates the butterfly stroke for a class in lifesaving techniques. The campus, one of nine in the statewide system, serves 10,000 students in the oceanside community of La Jolla, part of San Diego.*

His lab coat alight in afternoon sun, Jonas Salk pauses in the courtyard of the Salk Institute for Biological Studies in La Jolla. Dr. Salk developed the first polio vaccine, introduced in 1955. Five years later he came to southern California to build the research facility of his dreams, a place to gather "new 'hybrids' of science, people who can think productively in more than one area." The City of San Diego gave land for the institute. Home of many distinguished scientists, the area boasts six Nobel laureates, all but two in medicine or physiology (opposite, left to right): Harold C. Urey (chemistry), Francis Crick, Hannes Alfvén (physics), Renato Dulbecco, Roger Guillemin, Robert W. Holley. Dr. Urey and Dr. Alfvén work at the nearby University of California campus; the others serve there as professors but pursue their research at Salk.

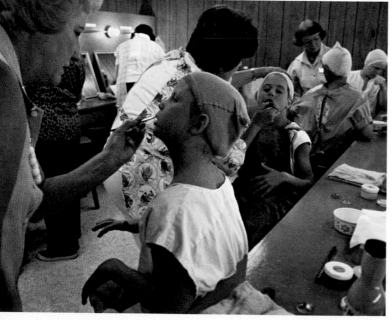

*L*ive models portray da Vinci's "Last Supper" in the annual Pageant of the Masters at Laguna Beach. The event stages more than 40 works of art with two casts totaling 300 volunteers, ages 4 to 78. They may hold a pose for as long as five minutes. "It takes a lot of stillness," said a small boy. Makeup (left) turns people into art. Gilded mortals portray the Ceres and Neptune of Cellini's famed golden saltcellar.

Man to man, ranch hand John Carey confers with 4-year-old Chad Quesenberry in the

working tack room of El Rancho Escondido: 600 acres of rolling hills on Santa Catalina island.   29

Teenagers at Huntington Beach, "the focal point of our social life," visit with lifeguard Bruce Cleeland on a warm, quiet November weekend. Guard stations, unused in the off season, stand in a row behind the jeep. Once the site of annual international surfing championships, renowned for its consistently ridable waves, mile-long Huntington Beach draws more than two and a half million people a year. Farther north at Manhattan Beach, another spot favored by surfers, Rena Herberts joins Walt Tomlinson beside the pier as he leaves the chilly waters of December.

nuggets, we call them, because they bring a premium price," he said. When all the lines were in, Joe estimated he had 300 pounds of fish—not a heavy haul for the work involved. "Just pin money," he said. "But we'd rather keep busy than sit around."

The catch varies, of course; and by dint of experience, skill, and hard work, Joe and Tony manage to do reasonably well. But small-boat fishermen, including those using nets, play a comparatively minor role in the overall San Diego fishing industry. The port is base for about 80 percent of California's distant-seas tuna fleet, which uses purse seines to net schools of yellowfin, bluefin, and skipjack tuna over a vast area extending to northern Chile.

One of the purse seiners was putting out to sea as we neared the familiar landmark of Point Loma and turned up the channel. The approach was busy at midday, with power cruisers and sailboats as well as military and commercial craft. As we headed for the dock under a bright blue sky, the bay and the city sparkled in the sun.

Half a mile from where the *Mary Ann* and *La Diana* usually tie up, just beyond a row of big tuna boats, a three-masted, square-rigged sailing ship hugs the wharf. She is the splendidly restored bark *Star of India*, oldest merchant vessel afloat and pride of the San Diego Maritime Museum.

Launched in 1863, the *Star* was based at San Francisco from 1902 to 1923. Each spring she sailed to Alaska's Bristol Bay, returning with salmon in the fall. Tony's father, Sicilian-born Vincenzo Giacalone, sailed on the *Star* in 1914 and again the next year. One Sunday afternoon he shared with me some of his vivid memories of those voyages.

"Once we got a big storm that lasted 25 hours," he said in his still-strong Italian accent. "Nobody could stay on deck.

The whole crew was below, except two men at the wheel, and they were tied to the bridge with a rope."

In 1920 Vincenzo and his wife, Caterina, also a native of Sicily, followed his brother to San Diego. "A nice, quiet town," he recalled. "Only two banks. And the fishermen walked right into the bank in their rubber boots."

For nearly 60 years the Giacalones have lived in the same neighborhood, a predominantly Italian district of well-kept houses and gardens. From there I drove Vincenzo, 85 and still active, to the waterfront to see his old ship. "I'm a seaman and fisherman all my life," he said proudly. As we topped a rise and the harbor came into view, he suddenly leaned forward. "Whenever I see the water, my heart jumps!"

SAN DIEGO and its suburbs form California's third largest metropolitan area, after those centered on the Los Angeles basin and San Francisco Bay. Its climate, even drier and more moderate in temperature than that of Los Angeles, and its spacious natural harbor have been the keys to its growth. It was a fishing town even before the Navy arrived. In 1901 a coaling station became the forerunner of what are literally dozens of naval installations that contribute heavily to the city's economy.

Today San Diego is famous as a military base, seaport, scientific research center, and focal point of higher education. Yet, despite these important activities, what San Diegans seem to take most seriously is recreation. There is widespread agreement that the mild climate and excellent facilities require a proper emphasis on leisure. No doubt this relaxed attitude contributes to the city's popularity with tourists.

San Diego boasts many parks and other recreational areas, but by far the largest are Balboa Park—with its

Free spirits frolic on Black's Beach, a secluded strand tucked among San Diego County's 70 miles of beaches. In 1977 public sentiment prevailed over city sanction of Black's as a nudist beach—formally acknowledged as "Swimsuit Optional" —but some well-tanned visitors still go home with highly localized sunburns.

botanical gardens, playing fields, theaters, museums, and incomparable zoo—and Mission Bay Park, a maze of lagoons, islands, and beaches, and home of Sea World's performing marine animals and its oceanographic exhibits.

With its bays and long ocean front, San Diego has no shortage of recreational shoreline. Some of its finest beaches lie to the north, below the seaward edge of the Torrey Pines mesa. The broken bluffs rise steeply to form an imposing, four-mile-long wall, 300 feet high in places, that extends from La Jolla almost to the racetrack-and-resort town of Del Mar.

At the base of the cliffs lies Torrey Pines State Beach, a flat, sandy shore that extends southward to city-owned Black's Beach. For several years Black's was famous as the only public beach in California where nudity was sanctioned by law—the official phrase was "Swimsuit Optional." In 1977 San Diego rescinded the ordinance.

The state beach is administered jointly with a state reserve that protects the distinctive Torrey pine trees and other native plants and wildlife—from sea figs to sumacs, gray foxes to great horned owls—atop the mesa and in the adjacent ravines and marshes.

To wander on a sharp winter day along the Torrey Pines beach is to discover a peaceful illusion of remote coastal wilderness. On one side loom the erosion-sculptured sandstone bluffs. On the other the foaming surf plays its endless, rhythmic game. Ahead stretch the damp, firm sands with their long horsewhips of kelp and ever-searching shorebirds. Except for airplanes overhead, the only sounds are the crash of the breakers and the insistent calls of wheeling sea gulls.

But if the beach below is quiet and uncrowded, a strip of ground at the top of the bluffs is at times one of the busiest spots on the coast. For the air above Torrey Pines can be ideal for a particular kind of flight: gliding and soaring on the air currents that sweep upward when ocean winds strike the abrupt barrier of cliffs. Sailplanes have climbed and

dipped and banked above the site for decades, and have been joined in recent years by radio-controlled models and hang gliders. On good days the air is full of colorful wings.

Because of its patterns of rising air, Torrey Pines is one of the few places where a hang-glider pilot can take off and land at the same level, avoiding the tedious climb back from a landing zone far below the departure point. But along with skill, the advanced pilots who use this port must have great patience. I spent several afternoons on the bluffs, and learned that the fliers devote many more hours to waiting than to flying. Much of the time either the wind is not strong enough or it is too strong; or it comes from the wrong direction; or clouds or fog blow in to obscure the flight zone and landing areas.

When everything is right, however, it is a thrill to watch a normally earthbound man or woman carry broad dacron wings—some span 36 feet—to the edge of the mesa, run two or three steps and leap into space, then rise like a great fanciful bird and start soaring back and forth along the cliffs. When ready to land, the flier turns inland, calls out, "Hang glider on final," then banks around and—if all goes well—touches down as lightly as a dandelion seed coming to rest.

Hang gliding was made possible by an airfoil considered for use in the space program, but was introduced to Americans as a sport by an adventurous Australian. It got an early start—about 1972—in California because of the state's particular combination of climate and terrain and, presumably, a receptive attitude toward the new and novel. Today 1,700 Californians are members of the U. S. Hang Gliding Association—25 percent of its total enrollment.

Among the fliers I talked with at Torrey Pines were two dedicated hang-glider pilots who are also partners in a related business venture.

Chuck Stahl, 50 ("Isn't that a heck of a name for a pilot?"), is a United Airlines captain with more than 10,000 hours of flying time. "I've found in hang gliding the excitement that got me interested in aviation in the first place," he said. "You feel pretty well removed from the dream of birdlike flight when you're sitting at the console of a 747."

Jeff Magnan, 19, Chuck's partner, has designed a new type of hang glider. Stahl has provided financial backing and is helping Jeff test and refine his design.

Chuck Stahl has no illusions about the safety problems; his son was killed several years ago while hang gliding. "I loved him very much, and I miss him," he said. He looked quickly away. "But I don't blame him, or the sport. He was doing something he loved, and he took a foolish chance—but no more foolish than some of the things I did when I was starting to fly. I got away with it, and he didn't. But now it's doubly important to me to do everything I can to make this sport as safe as possible."

The 300-foot cliffs of Torrey Pines are no place for a novice, so without much regret I had to forgo hang gliding. But I was eager for a different experience—my first sailplane ride.

Although I have been flying powered aircraft for many years as a private pilot, I had never been in a glider. One afternoon I climbed into the front seat of a graceful, slender-winged plane and was strapped in. A winch cable extending the length of the runway was hooked to the nose of the craft. Since the glider's landing gear is a single wheel, a helper stood at a wingtip to hold us level until we started our takeoff roll. After an errant patch of fog had floated past, pilot Larry Moore was ready. A flagman signaled the winch operator 1,200 feet away, and we were whisked down the runway and into the air. Quickly Larry released the cable, and we were on our own, 800 feet above the water.

For one accustomed to the noise of a powered plane, the silence of a glider comes as a pleasant surprise. I heard only the soft sounds of the air around us, and felt a rare sense of lightness, effortlessness, freedom.

Turning in a shallow bank, we looked down on low clouds just offshore. "We'll practice a spot landing," Larry said. In seconds we were only a few feet above the ground. Keeping up his air speed, he held the plane off, letting it rise and sink with the contours of the irregular landing field. "See that rubber cone ahead?" With that we touched down, rolling along on our single wheel until we nudged right up to the cone. The plane stopped and one wing slowly settled. A perfect landing.

I was hoping for another and longer flight, but just then the fog moved in again, and we had to give up for the day. As brief as my ride was, however, it made me understand the special appeal gliding and soaring have for many fliers.

THE ROAD leading to the Torrey Pines bluffs passes the entrance to the Salk Institute for Biological Studies. The structure, highly functional and severely handsome, was so awesome to my wife, Janice, that she called it "the most disturbing architecture I have ever seen." Four-story-tall wings of reinforced concrete, teakwood, and glass flank a large open court looking out to the Pacific.

Jonas Salk, developer of the first polio vaccine, came west rather skeptically in 1959 to look at this area on the advice of a colleague. "I didn't expect it to be an appropriate place for the kind of institute I had in mind," he told me. "I really came so I could say, 'I've looked at it, and now I'm going to move on.'" But he was captivated by what he found—positive community attitudes, a cluster of other educational and research institutions, the climate. And soon after his visit, the City of San Diego offered the choice 27-acre Torrey Pines site.

The designer of the building was Louis I. Kahn. "I went to him to ask how to pick an architect," Dr. Salk said. "I never got an answer." But he got an architect; Kahn himself promptly became interested in Salk's ideas, and the two formed a close working relationship.

"Our ideas kept evolving," Salk continued. "I gradually learned enough architecture from Louis Kahn to make the right critical comments."

Now age 64, the center's founding

35

director concentrates on writing and research. But he emphasizes that his laboratory group is only one of 17 at the Salk Institute, whose investigations range from the transmission of hereditary characteristics to the chemical bases of human behavior. Most of his writing is done in the very early hours of morning. "My biggest problem is in managing my time," he said. "As I get older I find there is more and more I want to do, rather than less and less."

NORTH OF TORREY PINES and Del Mar the coast highway settles into a pattern, alternately skirting white beaches and threading palm- and eucalyptus-shaded resort communities and their ever-growing residential subdivisions. Sometimes the beach parks and adjacent towns share the same colorful names: Cardiff by the Sea, Leucadia, Carlsbad.

Then, just beyond Oceanside, the pattern is interrupted. Here the U. S. Marine Corps is landlord of a 17-mile stretch of the Sunset Coast, the ocean edge of 125,000-acre Camp Pendleton. Inland from the beachfront, grassland and chaparral-covered foothills rise rapidly toward the mountains. Although Marines are better known for shooting up the landscape than for preserving it, I found them admirably sensitive to their stewardship of a huge piece of undeveloped land in the midst of one of the most rapidly growing urban regions in the United States. Camp Pendleton has an enviable record of enlightened management of natural resources, ranging from recycling of its water supply to soil conservation and protection of wildlife.

Base officials are particularly proud of the story of the least tern, an endangered species. Tank-tread impressions in the sand, someone discovered, make ideal nesting places for this small seabird. By putting certain beach maneuver areas off limits during the nesting season, the Marines have helped the least tern to increase steadily in number.

When not in use for amphibious training, many of the landing beaches are opened to public recreational use; and a six-mile section of the north Pendleton shoreline is now administered as a park by special agreement between the Marine Corps and the State.

In addition to the beaches at Camp Pendleton, the island of San Clemente, 61 miles off the coast—one of the eight Channel Islands—is available to the Marines and Navy for training operations. In early February 1978, the 57-square-mile island was the target of a raid by an air-sea-land team during a major training exercise I was invited to observe.

The day before the landing, I went by helicopter from Pendleton to the island. It was already the scene of preliminary action. The invading force had put ashore reconnaissance teams; some of the men had been captured. When the attack came, well before dawn the next day, the first strike was by a helicopter-borne force hitting high ground at the waist of the island. In the dark I could trace the parade of circling choppers by their flashing red beacons. Then gradually, through the dusky first light, I could make out the troopships standing offshore. Soon a column of amtracs—amphibious tracked vehicles—moved toward the beach, following a narrow channel through kelp beds. As the amtracs rolled ashore, squads of riflemen and machine gun and mortar crews scrambled down the ramps and into position behind a ridge of sand.

More raiders came, then more, in a growing din of gunfire. Though the fire was sound without substance, one defensive action sent the invaders clutching for their gas masks. As a cloud of tear gas spread along the beach, I retreated, coughing and gasping, up the steep embankment toward the mask I had, of course, neglected to carry with me.

Except for that brief recess, I spent the morning in the midst of the action on the beachhead. During a lull I asked one of the raiders, Sgt. Garry Watkins, about the morale of his rifle squad. "After two weeks at sea, we're just glad to be back on solid ground," he said. A driver whose jeep was stuck in the sand exclaimed cheerfully, "I keep thinking it's nice no one's really shooting at me."

Late that afternoon I flew over the island on my way back to Camp Pendleton. As the helicopter climbed I could see some of the riflemen, still with several days of grueling action ahead, looking up at us, and I could imagine their expressions of weariness and envy.

Off to the left a few minutes later I could see another of the Channel Islands, that loosely scattered cluster of eight offshore mountaintops rising out of the Pacific. Santa Catalina is near enough to the mainland—only 22 miles—to be visible on a clear day, yet far enough away to be tantalizing. For generations it has been one of California's most-visited tourist destinations, and there is daily service by both sea and air. The blue harbor, red tile roofs, and subtropical plantings of Avalon, its single town, suggest a Mediterranean port. Shops and cafes line its few downtown streets, and stuccoed houses climb the hills just beyond. Not the least of its attractions are the big bands that still play at the famed Casino Ballroom.

But of equal appeal is the wilderness quality of the rest of the island, as I discovered later during a tortuous tour of the island's back roads. The low, rugged mountains are largely covered with chaparral, but groves of trees in canyons and on lower slopes include island oak, Catalina cherry, and the rare Catalina ironwood, found nowhere else.

Four hundred bison—a herd that got its start from a small group left by a movie company—roam the island, wild boar and deer thrive, and red-tailed hawks glide overhead. Now hundreds of species of plant and animal life will be permanently protected. To ensure perpetuation of this primitive area, the Santa Catalina Island Company in 1975 transferred most of the island's 76 square miles to a conservancy organized to preserve the property. It was one of the largest such gifts on record.

Preservation of another kind, of the quiet cloisters and vine-covered ruins of Mission San Juan Capistrano, draws a steady stream of visitors to a green coastal valley in southern Orange County. But on March 19, St. Joseph's Day, the stream becomes a flood: In 1978 25,000 visitors crowded into the small town to welcome the swallows that return to the mission each spring.

Laguna Beach, ten miles northwest of Capistrano, is a pleasant town of steep hills, gardens, and cliff-protected coves whose white sand beaches contrast with the dark, rugged rocks just offshore. Quiet in the winter, it caps its lively summer season each July and August with a Festival of Arts that has grown into perhaps the biggest event of its kind anywhere.

The festival was begun 46 years ago to help an artists' colony drawn to Laguna Beach by its surpassing beauty, and the emphasis is still on local work. About 175 men and women, preselected by jury, display paintings, sculpture, handicrafts, and photography.

On a typical day the six acres of exhibition grounds are aswarm with visitors. Some artists are at work in their booths, others are deep in conversation, others sit quietly and watch the reactions of those passing by. There is color and motion on all sides, and the crowds keep coming. In seven weeks an estimated 300,000 people visit the show.

But the most memorable part of the festival is the Pageant of the Masters, in which the art of *tableaux vivants* has been brought to perfection. The living reproductions of famous paintings, sculptures, and other works of art, created by meticulously costumed men and women and boys and girls of the area, are startling in their vividness and accuracy. Forty or so scenes are presented, and in each the models hold their poses for as long as five minutes. There are often old favorites like "Pinkie" and "The Blue Boy," and traditionally the final picture is da Vinci's "Last Supper."

Between Laguna Beach and Corona del Mar, the inquisitive stranger spies a puzzling gap in the long urban strip that extends northward from Camp Pendleton. Abruptly, instead of houses and shopping centers, there is a 3 1/2-mile stretch of sparsely developed coastline. This is the southwestern edge of the 77,000-acre Irvine Ranch, put together a century ago by James Irvine from old Spanish-Mexican land-grant properties. For decades the ranch remained a huge agricultural enclave, leapfrogged by subdivisions as the Los Angeles metropolitan area grew. In the early 1960's cautious development began, with designation of a future town of Irvine, establishment of the University of California at Irvine, and the beginnings of extensive residential and commercial construction. But most of the ranch, 60,000 acres, is still in agricultural use.

Today, the master plan evolved for the ranch calls for special treatment of a 10,000-acre coastal parcel. Part of it—including the 3 1/2 miles of beaches and bluff tops—would be made available for sale to an appropriate agency for preservation as open space. Some opponents of the plan want all, not most, of the parcel preserved. So far, the State of California hopes to purchase 3,170 acres for parkland.

"Everybody likes open space, but no one can afford it," Martin Brower of the Irvine Company told me. The company leases some land for a stable, a trailer park, and other concessions, but it must bear the heavy cost of property taxes and other expenses on the parcel, "and we can't do that forever," he said.

The Irvine Ranch contains the last large tract of coastal land still in its natural state between southern Orange and western Ventura counties. Starting at Corona del Mar, development crowds to the water's edge, and the coast becomes a tightly knit fabric of apartment complexes, beach cottages on small lots, and marinas thick with the masts of sailboats and the trappings of power cruisers. Water-oriented shopping centers flank power plants and public beaches. Here and there are community trademarks. A diminutive auto ferry still links the beach homes of peninsular Balboa with the shop-lined streets of Balboa Island. And at Huntington Beach oil wells dot the shoreline and the town, the pumps dipping their necks ceaselessly like great birds foraging for grain. Behind my motel, on a plot of ground barely large enough for a vegetable garden, a well pumped away steadily—and had been doing so, I was told, since 1930.

The distinctive smell of oil-tinged salt air, first noticeable near Huntington Beach, pervades the coast for miles northward. Approaching Seal Beach, the highway traverses a forest of tall derricks, many of them decades old.

Oil has affected both southern California's landscape and its economy since the first strikes in Los Angeles in 1892. But the great boom came much later, first with a massive field at Huntington Beach in 1920, then another on Signal Hill near Long Beach in 1921.

The famed hill, still an unmistakable if unlovely landmark, proved one of the richest of all California's oil fields. But today the area's principal production comes from offshore wells. Disguised as apartment towers, the derricks reflect a strikingly different attitude toward aesthetics than does the time-honored eyesore of Signal Hill.

Someone has called Long Beach "Iowa with palm trees." For whatever reason, the city has attracted a large proportion of Midwesterners, and 25,000 Iowans have been known to show up for the annual Iowa Picnic here. Many streets are lined with small, single-family dwellings reminiscent of working-class neighborhoods in the Midwest.

When I turned onto Ocean Boulevard, I saw houses ahead that were much larger—though many of these stately old homes with their broad porches were also suggestive of the Midwest. But I was looking for something else, across the street and beyond the landscaped promenade, out across the water. I got a glimpse of her, and then a full view. From the place of honor created after her retirement from the sea, the fine old liner *Queen Mary* dominates the Long Beach waterfront.

I gazed at the majestic vessel, now a hotel, convention center, and maritime museum, and recalled the welcome she received here in 1967, at the end of her last great cruise from Southampton. I had boarded her at Acapulco for the last leg of that journey, and was on the bridge the morning of December 9 when it seemed that every small craft in southern California—10,000 was the estimate!—came to escort us into port.

No longer profitable as a passenger ship in the age of jet aircraft, the *Queen Mary* was bought by the City of Long Beach to serve as a tourist attraction. She has certainly been that, but the cost of conversion so far exceeded estimates that she became a local political issue. Critics pushed for her sale. But in the spring of 1978, city officials declared her financial picture improved and reaffirmed their determination to make her a profitable enterprise.

Eric Kamien, curator of exhibits, gave me a tour of depths of the ship few people see, and I gained a new awe of her vast size and complexity. British actress Beatrice Lillie made the point best when she asked: "What time does this place get to England?"

Kamien has been working aboard the *Queen Mary* for five years, and is still discovering things. "It's like a continuing treasure hunt," he said. "We locate an unknown compartment, or open a locked door, and find another cache of ship's supplies or more records. Who knows? Maybe someday we can reconstruct a detailed account of her entire career."

FOR ONCE luck was with us on the weather. It had been raining for weeks in southern California, one storm after another bringing gale warnings for seafarers. But on the day I went in search of gray whales on their early spring migration from Baja California northward to the Bering Sea, I was met with bright sunshine and relatively smooth seas.

Relatively, I emphasize, for many of my shipmates found them not quite smooth enough. Aboard the *Californian* on an excursion sponsored by the Cabrillo Marine Museum in San Pedro were several dozen schoolchildren. At the outset they were as bright in spirit as the varied colors of their warm jackets. All was well as we churned out of Long Beach Harbor, through a gate in the breakwater and into the open sea.

But then the *Californian* began to ride the waves with a pronounced pitch and roll. One by one the casualties mounted. A sympathetic teacher guiding a pale boy or girl would make her way aft and position her charge at the end of a growing row of youngsters kneeling abjectly at the stern. Eventually, the invalids would exchange their places at the rail for space on the deck, stretching out or curling up in melancholy surrender.

Meanwhile the hardier children clung to the rails eagerly keeping watch for whales. Soon the skipper spotted one and called out its position. Along with half a dozen other boats, we converged on a patch of ocean marked every few minutes by the spouting of a whale or by its arching leap as it cleared the water, then waved its tail as it crashed back into the sea.

Each sighting brought a cheer from the young observers. Precisely at noon, as if saluting the midday hour, four whales arched high in unison in a performance as flawless as anything offered by their trained killer-whale cousins at Sea World and Marineland.

After an hour of repeated sightings we turned toward port. Ralph, 7, told me that he "saw about 16 or 22 whales." Tavia and Jennifer, both 5, said the whales were even larger than they had expected. "They were *real* big," said Jennifer. "Yikes! I'm glad we came!"

The teacher, surveying the limp forms on the deck, was not so sure. When a third-grader hurried up to ask, "When can we eat lunch?" she looked slightly panicky. "Not," she said firmly, "for a long time."

"To many the shoreline is irresistible"

TUCKED INTO the south-facing crescent of San Pedro Bay, the twin harbors of Los Angeles and Long Beach are protected from the open sea by the world's longest breakwater, nine miles overall. The ports form a bustling complex of naval and commercial shipping facilities, fish canneries, and pleasure-boat marinas. To the sounds of whistles, bells, and tugboat engines, ships of more than 50 nations move through a maze of basins and channels. A towering suspension bridge, giant cranes, and oil tanks shape the skyline, overlooking row upon row of docks lined with cargo vessels.

The harbor area never sleeps. Floodlights often burn all night on freighter decks and along broad wharves designed for efficient handling of bulk products, or automobiles, or big containers that can be lifted directly from ship to rail car or motor truck.

Man, not nature, was the principal creator of this harbor. A century ago, with Los Angeles beginning to burgeon 20 inland miles to the north, foresighted leaders recognized the need to develop a deepwater port for the city. Engineers recommended the marshy anchorage at San Pedro as the site, to be enlarged and deepened by dredging and sheltered by a long breakwater. But influential owners of Santa Monica property challenged the choice, and a long political struggle began. Eventually the necessary federal subsidy went to San Pedro; and Los Angeles assured itself a port by extending its city limits down a long, narrow corridor to the San Pedro-Wilmington waterfront. Long Beach began developing its own port alongside.

For nearly 50 years Nate DiBiasi has known this growing, changing waterfront intimately. He exemplifies one version of the American dream—the immigrant laborer who achieves a position of prominence and major responsibility. In 1973 he became the first longshoreman to serve on the Los Angeles Board of Harbor Commissioners, appointed by another man who had risen through the ranks: Tom Bradley, a black former police officer who has twice been elected mayor of the nation's third largest city.

Except for World War II service in the South Pacific, DiBiasi has lived in the harbor area since he was 14, a year after arriving in California from Italy. As a boy he spent non-school hours on the passenger piers handling baggage for tips. As soon as he was old enough, he went to work on the freight docks part-time, and after the war he became a longshoreman. Automation of cargo handling was still far in the future, and Nate recalls vividly how hard the job could be.

"Just about everything that used to be done by *(Continued on page 65)*

Vintage cars in a Santa Monica showroom surround vendor Donald Williams.
His firm, now based inland at Toluca Lake, leases autos for movie and television productions
and sells them to buffs, collectors, and investors alert to their rapidly rising value.

Huge man-made harbor, the Port of Los Angeles handles more than 3,000 ships a year. Nate DiBiasi (left) became a harbor commissioner after 28 years as a longshoreman here. In neighboring Long Beach Harbor, disguised derricks on an "oil island" tap one of the largest producing fields in California.

*Catamarans in confusion contend with light air before the start of a race off San Pedro—
"a mess," said one participant. Racers returning from the Humphrey Bogart Series glide past
California sea lions resting on a buoy at the entrance to Newport Bay. Three and a half miles long,
the bay shelters more than 9,000 boats, from spacious yachts to dinghies. Not merely a
pastime, boating amounts to a passion for many who sail here year round. Yet even
a spectacular regatta may go unnoticed by people in town, because intense development along
the shore has virtually walled off the ocean from street-level view.*

Converging on southern California, top athletes train all year in the mild climate. Bicyclists, Olympic hopefuls among them, speed down city streets in the 100-kilometer Manhattan Beach Grand Prix. Body-builders in Santa Monica await the judges' decision for the title of Mr. America. Like many other enthusiasts, Pete Grymkowski— Mr. World of 1977—moved to California to train at Gold's Gym. "It was and is still the Mecca of body-building," he says. "I'm not trying to sell anyone on the idea, but it gives both female and male the chance to excel and find self-respect."

48

After a day at the shore, bus patrons wait for their ride in front of a mural of a Santa Monica beach scene. One of 150-plus commissioned by the Los Angeles Citywide Mural Project, it depicts the now-destroyed Pacific Ocean Park in the early 1900's. Murals throughout California reflect the state's ethnic diversity and help foster community pride. Enjoying themselves and the music, spirited partners dance at the Santa Monica Senior Recreation Center in Palisades Park. At left, Gebel "the daredevil cat" leaps through a ring of fire during a Los Angeles performance of the traveling Royal Lichtenstein Quarter-Ring Sidewalk Circus. Two members of the three-man staff urge him on. Nick Weber, self-described "clown and priest and Jesuit," manages the show; he also eats fire, tells jokes, and walks a tightrope. The priest calls the circus his ministry. It mixes magic and animal tricks with fables advocating honesty, kindness, and simplicity.

49

Californians adapt to living on the edge of a continent—and on the verge of disaster.
Homes perched on 150-foot bluffs of the Palos Verdes Peninsula (above) command
magnificent views and price tags approaching a million dollars. Located in a relatively
stable area of the southern California coast, these houses face less danger from earthquakes
and sliding land than do others nearby. Only a few miles away, a resident of the Portuguese
Bend section adjusts jacks under his house: a routine chore. Since 1956 the land and
the house have slipped 95 feet toward the ocean. Heavy rains can double the
rate of slippage. One geologist quipped grimly, "Wait long enough and he will have
beachfront property." Fencing from a Malibu homesite comes to rest at the end of
its plunge down a steep hillside. Torrential winter rains in 1978 caused landslides and
mudflows in Malibu and on hills and mountains denuded by summer fires.

52

Flames engulf Sycamore Canyon during the 1977 Santa Barbara fire, touched off accidentally when a kite short-circuited power lines. The dryness of brush after a two-year drought, plus high temperatures and low humidity, helped the fire spread swiftly, destroying 234 homes. Erratic winds whipped flames that leveled one house, yet left its neighbor unharmed. Below, some of the 1,100 fire fighters and 116 fire engines that battled the blaze await reassignment to other sectors of the line.

Walking an Irish wolfhound in the shade of eucalyptus trees, a young woman strolls down a driveway on an oceanfront farm in Hope Ranch, a community west of Santa Barbara. At the Hope Ranch Riding Club, owners prepare purebred horses for shows throughout the country; handler Jenny Hirsch and champion hunter Demetrius stand under an archway of the main building. Trumpet vines climb the white stucco to the clay tile roof, Spanish motifs like those of many buildings in Santa Barbara. Since 1769, when friars began founding missions along the coast, Spanish influence has marked the life of the region. In Montecito, an eastern suburb, Frank Ruiz pauses before a bullfight poster hanging in the oldest structure on the San Ysidro Ranch, an adobe house built in 1825. He grew up and still works at the guest ranch his father supervised from 1896 to 1946.

Attired in traditional kimono, artist Yasu Eguchi kneels in the living room of his home near Santa Barbara. A straw and seaweed raincape and hat—Oriental farmer's dress—hang on the wall behind him. For his home, Eguchi chose a coastal site with vistas of ocean and mountains reminiscent of his native Japan. His work reflects the forms he finds in nature. Inspired by bits of moss growing on a rock, crystal droplets of water, or clusters of wild flowers, Eguchi creates elegant landscapes like the watercolor above, "Early Spring." Painted on handmade rice paper, it combines the disciplined techniques of Japanese calligraphy and the freer style of abstract art. Intense and thoughtful, Eguchi describes the painting as "a recollection of a Japanese spring with a California landscape—looking through wild mustard flowers to an orchard."

Viewed *from the top of an oil rig in the Santa Barbara Channel, 30-foot sections of pipe seem to shrink to pencil size. Roughnecks working on one of 14 oil platforms in the channel pull drill pipe from a well.*

A major spill here in 1969 and growing environmental concerns resulted in tightened offshore drilling regulations, but the search for oil goes on.

FOLLOWING PAGES: *90° F. weather in late November delights surfers at Rincon Point, between Santa Barbara and Ventura. The perfect curl of the waves in winter makes this an ideal beach for surfing then.*

59

Packing his son along, biologist George
Antonelis photographs sea lions as he records their
numbers on San Miguel island. Many zoologists
consider this the most important observation
site along the West Coast because the island supports
six different species of seals; five of them breed here.
The National Park Service and the National
Marine Fisheries Service study and attempt to
preserve both the animals and their habitats.
A solitary California sea lion pauses near the water's
edge. At left, a sea lion pup finds a comfortable
alternative to its usual rocky perch: a convenient
young northern elephant seal. In summer most
male elephant seals molt; sometimes, says Antonelis,
they lie stationary so long that adult
male sea lions use the huge "living rocks" as
territorial boundary markers.

a strong back is now done by machines," he said. "Automation cost us a lot of jobs, but it lengthened the lives of those who were still working. You used to start a ship and work until it was finished. If it took 30 hours, that was how long you kept going. And some of the cargo! Maybe stinking raw hides, full of mice, maggots, and flies. The hardest to handle were bales of rubber; they were heavy, and they'd stick together. And cotton. Two men would wrestle a 550-pound bale and try to stand it up on the uneven flooring, banging their heads on the I-beams."

DiBiasi is a loyal member of the International Longshoremen's and Warehousemen's Union. "West Coast longshoremen split off from the A.F.L. in 1948 and worked out a new agreement with the Pacific Maritime Association," he said. "Our contract provides for settlement of labor-management disputes by compulsory arbitration during the life of the agreement. Since 1948 we've only had one dock strike out here—four and a half months all told."

Commissioner DiBiasi takes pride in the success of the Port of Los Angeles, which consistently moves more tonnage than any other Pacific Coast port. The harbor commissioners operate the huge facility as a self-supporting city department. "Not only do we use no tax funds," Nate pointed out, "we make a large contribution every year to the city's general fund."

A LTHOUGH the southeast side of the Palos Verdes Peninsula is occupied by urban, industrial San Pedro, the rest of the peninsula is made up of communities in an almost rural setting. Across the slopes curve bridle trails and white-fenced lanes shaded by lacy-foliaged peppertrees and tall, pungent eucalyptus. Favored with clear air and abundant sunshine, the peninsula is generally considered one of the most desirable places to live in southern California—except for one part of a residential area called Portuguese Bend. That section is relentlessly inching toward the sea.

The most dramatic earth movements are sudden and violent—earthquakes, avalanches, mudflows. At Portuguese Bend I saw the results of something much more gradual and less frightening but equally insistent, and met some of the people who have come to terms with it.

Geologists call the phenomenon a "block-glide," which occurs in sloping layered rocks; the slowly moving surface layer slides down the stable rock beneath it. Here the movement ranges from one to six inches a month. "It's like living on a glacier," one resident told me.

His situation is worse than that of most of his neighbors, whose houses at least are moving as units. "In our case, sections of ground under the house are actually stretching in different directions, so there's a wrenching effect," he explained. The foundation long ago became distorted and useless, and the house now sits on heavy blocks, timbers, and jacks. The owner adjusts the jacks every couple of weeks to keep the main structure level. But there is no way to keep everything aligned, so the garage, porches, patio, and entry stairs tilt at odd angles, a bit like the crooked house at an amusement park.

Portuguese Bend was developed as a residential area in the late 1940's and early '50's. When the ground started slipping in 1956—triggered, the courts decided, by the county's work on a new road across the hills—about 200 houses were affected, 65 in this immediate neighborhood. The rest of the area has remained relatively stable.

Many of the houses were damaged

Her grin unquenched by a downpour, a resident wades across a mud-clogged Malibu driveway. Prolonged winter rains in 1978, and resulting mudslides, repeatedly blocked the Pacific Coast Highway. One jokester placed a "For Sale" sign in the middle of the pavement—a prank inspired by the skyrocketing costs of Malibu real estate.

beyond repair and have been demolished; one sits vacant. But six of the original owners still occupy their homes, and 26 other families—fully aware of the problems—have bought damaged houses and moved in, convinced that bargain prices and pleasant surroundings were sufficient to offset the obvious difficulties. Some have undergirded their houses with steel framing that holds the structures firmly together.

Adjustments have been necessary in public utilities. Coiled springs connect overhead wires to supporting poles; water and gas lines are laid aboveground and fitted with expansion joints.

But even in a house as tugged and counter-tugged as my host's, "It's all in getting used to it," he said. And his wife added, "Once you stop worrying about things like cracks in the plaster, or the absence of parallel lines and right angles, you can be quite comfortable. This is really a delightful area, with its country atmosphere. We haven't found any place we like as well—so why move?"

Meanwhile, the terrain slowly changes—an evolving canyon here, a new escarpment there. And every few weeks, down on the main road, a county crew smooths out the asphalt and repaints the double yellow center stripe where a widening zigzag marks the edge of the slide zone.

SEVERAL MILES WEST of Portuguese Bend, I turned down the long sloping driveway leading to Marineland of the Pacific. The park was closed for major construction and refurbishing after a change of ownership, but its marine animals remained as trainees-in-residence and were keeping the staff busy. "We've found they really miss the audiences—they get noticeably listless," said Tom Otten, the oceanarium's curator of mammals, "and we have to give them a lot of attention to make up for it."

A young woman named Ann Brierton guided me past sea lions, elephant seals, dolphins, otters, and other marine mammals, mostly youngsters that had been stranded on nearby beaches and rescued by the Marineland staff.

"We get several such calls almost every week," Ann said, "perhaps eight or ten a week in the spring. If we get there in time, we haul them in, treat them for injuries and other ailments, then try to help them along until they're strong enough to go back into the ocean or to another oceanarium.

"Here's Spike—a baby sea lion we had to bottle-feed at first."

Then she led me upstairs to an amphitheater where I watched trainers Jill Stratton and Gary Fox work with a killer whale named Orky, star of the Marineland cast. Competing with Jill's whistle, the splashing of a five-ton body on the pool surface, and music from the public-address system, Tom talked about the challenges and rewards of dealing with these animals.

"It's hard to overemphasize how intelligent they are," he said. "We have to be very alert to their psychological well-being. If they're treated in a demeaning way, they get depressed, and they're less resistant to disease. They can even get ulcers!"

I asked if there was a significant hazard in working so intimately with the powerful killer whales.

"As long as the trainers are fair and consistent with them, there's really not much danger," Tom replied. "Sometimes they just don't want you around, and they'll make it clear they'd like you out of the pool. But I don't think they'd ever deliberately hurt anybody."

Just then Orky gave a great leap and splashed what seemed like half the water in the tank onto a cluster of onlookers. Then Jill climbed on his back and rode off at high speed. "It's playtime," Tom announced. "As I said, it's quite a challenge to keep the animals happy while the place is closed down. They really miss the crowds!"

North of the Palos Verdes Peninsula the broad, sandy strands begin again, and public beaches stretch along most of the Los Angeles County coastline, interrupted by marinas, airport runways, and intrusions of industry. Altogether the county's Department of Beaches administers more than 40 miles of state, county, and municipal beach property, used in 1977 by an estimated 60 million visitors.

County officials are particularly proud of the department's corps of lifeguards. There are about 620 of these, of whom 120 are career guards. Despite the millions of visitors, drownings on guarded beaches have totaled only seven over the last decade.

Beach use is heaviest in warm weather, of course, but to many the shoreline is irresistible the year around. On chill, gray days, beach lovers simply put on more clothes. I remember two fishermen on a windswept pier—ages perhaps 5 and 7—encased in complete nor'easter rain gear, one in bright yellow and the other in royal blue.

The climate of the California coast is one of distinct wet and dry seasons. Almost all significant rainfall comes between early October and late May. If the winter rains fail, a dry year is inevitable.

In December 1977, California was into the third year of one of the worst droughts in memory. Many communities were rationing water, farmers and ranchers faced serious problems, and the tinderbox conditions had contributed to several calamitous fires in residential, grassland, and forest areas.

Then the rains came—and kept coming. By February 1978 much of the state already had received twice the normal annual precipitation, as measured from July 1 to June 30. The worst storms brought flooding, wind damage, and devastating mudslides, especially in the burned-over areas. Homes were destroyed in several communities when heavy surf and abnormally high tides undermined oceanfront sites.

In January and February I drove through some of the heaviest rains I have ever seen—once it took more than five hours to cover 90 miles on open freeway. And all one night I thought the howling winds would surely blow away a large, clanging sign outside my motel room. The sign held, but next morning I discovered that much of a large public pier just down the road had been carried out to sea.

But the beach enthusiasts are never put off for long. On a bright, brisk day after one of the storms, with the sun catching countless diamonds on the water, I found Redondo Beach well populated. Shopkeepers were doing a lively business along the pier's International Boardwalk. There were cyclists on the paths and sailboats offshore, picnickers on the sand and strollers near the water; wading dogs, a soaring kite, a new volleyball net; and even a swimmer: 40 yards out, a ruddy, white-haired man stroked away steadily.

Later, from palm-lined Palisades Park atop the bluffs at Santa Monica, I looked down on another busy beach and the city's famous amusement pier—soon to be renovated, merry-go-round and all. Santa Monica, easily reached by freeway from all of Los Angeles, is by far the area's most heavily used beach. In 1977 it had 13.7 million visitors, nearly one-fourth of the total for the entire county coast!

As I stood watching the scene below, I realized that the last three or four couples to stroll past had all been conversing in Spanish. Despite California's Spanish-Mexican heritage, English has been the dominant language ever since the gold rush of 1849. But with new emphasis on ethnic pride, and significant numbers of Puerto Ricans and other Hispanics joining the Mexican-Americans in the Spanish-speaking population—not to mention the continuing influx of illegal aliens—the state is becoming increasingly bilingual.

A short distance from the park, a glass-fronted corner building housed one of southern California's more unusual business enterprises. Browsing through the showroom of Automotive Classics was like returning to the days when motorcar designers made sure their products were distinctive, and almost any schoolboy could tell an auto's make and year from two blocks away. Here I encountered such classics as an immaculate Model A Ford, a dignified Duesenberg, a supercharged Graham, and an elegant Cord, all restored to their condition of 30 or 40 years ago.

The owner of this unofficial museum where everything was for sale was Don Williams, a young man with blond hair and a friendly smile who turned his interest in old cars into a highly successful business. His restored automobiles are in demand not only by collectors and other buyers but also by commercial renters—a filmmaker bringing a 1930's street to life, an advertising agency preparing a television spot or a record jacket that requires photographing an automobile from another era.

Actually, Williams said, he has been acquiring many things from an earlier day, from furniture to slot machines. "I'll collect anything that's older than I am," he laughed. He hopes someday to have a display room that will be a showcase of nostalgia, furnished and decorated to evoke the two or three decades before World War II.

The likelihood of my becoming a restored-car customer looked slim. As long as I can remember, I have wanted a Model A roadster. Don had a beauty, and I priced it. Alas, I was almost as far from being able to afford it as on the day I took my first ride in a rumble seat—when I was in kindergarten.

As Santa Monica Bay curves west, the coast highway follows, separating the long, flat beach from shrubby hills slashed by wooded canyons. This is fabled Malibu, home of film stars and other celebrities but equally known as one of California's finest surfing areas. Clusters of expensive houses look out on battalions of surfers almost every day of the year.

Beyond the cliffs of Point Mugu, the land flattens into the delta of the Santa Clara River. Here orange and lemon groves alternate with avocado orchards and tall windbreaks of eucalyptus and tamarisk trees.

Oxnard and Ventura, though both are growing, seem quiet after the ceaseless traffic of metropolitan Los Angeles. Ventura, the name almost universally used, is a short form. The full name of the city, as well as of its historic mission, is San Buenaventura.

North of town the highway stays close to the coast as it winds past the flower fields of Carpinteria and a series of offshore oil platforms. Ahead, rising sharply from Santa Barbara's coastal shelf, loom the Santa Ynez Mountains.

Santa Barbara, Californians generally acknowledge, has a flavor all its own. It is far enough north to avoid the orbit of Los Angeles, far enough south to share the warm, relatively dry Mediterranean climate. Proud of its twin-towered "Queen of the Missions," it has translated a Spanish colonial heritage into a pervasive architectural style that wears well with subtropical groves and gardens. It is a university town, a habitat of artists, writers, and musicians, a refuge of affluent retirees. In its distinctive setting it backs against tall mountains and looks out on blue ocean.

For such a normally quiet, almost serene community, Santa Barbara has undergone some traumatic misfortunes. Little more than half a century ago it was crippled by one of California's most damaging earthquakes. In the late 1960's, the peace of its University of California campus was shattered by political bombings, a rash of other violent crimes, and clashes between police and student radicals. Early in 1969 the West Coast's worst oil spill occurred in the Santa Barbara Channel when an offshore well shaft ruptured.

In July of 1977, a kite short-circuited power lines, and the sparks ignited dry grass and chaparral. The flames were fanned by the notorious hot, dry Santa Ana winds that sometimes blast into southern California from the high desert—and before the inferno was contained three days later, 234 homes had been destroyed.

A few weeks after the fire, my wife, Janice, and I drove through the burned-over area. What struck us forcefully was not just the extent of the destruction but also the capriciousness of the flames. Spread by wind-borne sparks as well as ground fire, the blaze had leapfrogged here and there, leaving a house or several houses unscathed in the midst of a block of charred ruins.

Fortunately, no fatalities resulted

from that grim episode, and within a few months many of the victims were already resolutely rebuilding.

Then, on August 13, 1978, a sharp earthquake shook Santa Barbara. Damage was widespread but fairly light. Again, the prompt response was to get about the business of cleaning up.

Such a reaction was only natural in a city known both for determined individualism and a strong sense of community. That spirit had been demonstrated after every previous disaster, but it is apparent also in the routine life of Santa Barbara—in the protection and beautification of its waterfront, citizen participation in public events and celebrations, political involvement, and traditions such as the informal Sunday exhibits by local artists and craftsmen along oceanside Cabrillo Boulevard.

Interested in art, hospitable to artists, the city has been the home of many of them over the years. The work of one distinguished professional—Yasu Eguchi—particularly intrigued me, and I called on him one warm spring afternoon to learn more about the man behind the paintings. As we talked, I began to discern the remarkable detachment of an observer who is trying to fathom not only the visual world and a still-foreign society but himself as well.

"I have been in the United States more than ten years now," he told me. "I met my wife in Japan when she was teaching there. She was the first American I had ever met. Frankly, I did not expect to like anything American."

Although Eguchi was already an established painter in Japan, he considers his move to the United States a critical step in his artistic development. "When I came to this country, it opened my eyes," he said. "There is so much happening. There are so many different kinds of people. At first I was bewildered. But I was fortunate in visiting many places—the East, the Deep South, as well as the West—and that helped me to understand."

Yasu originally came to Santa Barbara because it is the home of his wife's family, but he has found it suits him well. "I am very much at home here," he said. "With the mountains and the sea, it reminds me of my native Kyushu island. And it is so cosmopolitan; it is a good place for someone interested in more than one country, and in more than one culture."

Eguchi's creative touch is evident everywhere at his hillside home. I saw it in the design of the entry garden with its elevated deck, tall bamboo, and soft sound of falling water; in the white walls and dark wood of rooms built around his handmade Japanese furnishings; in his whimsical metal-and-wire sculptures, including a unicyclist somehow suggesting Don Quixote, and a figure of Saint Francis, bird in hand, fabricated from a discarded Volkswagen muffler ("these are my recreation"). But, of course, his paintings are his life.

The examples to be seen in his house represent several approaches and techniques, some as disparate as collages, others tightly disciplined landscapes. He paints on rice paper, mostly in watercolor.

Part of the fascination of his work is in the distinctly Oriental tone his techniques give even to non-Oriental scenes. "I guess I see everything in a kind of double image that is combined in my painting," he said.

"Visually this is so rich and varied a country, it had to have an enormous effect on me. Still, my subconscious is steeped in what I knew as a child. In that sense I am still Japanese, although after ten years I consider myself American. No, not American . . . artistically, at least, I am just myself, not Japanese or American or anything else."

ABOUT TO LEAVE southern California at the end of one visit, I sat in late evening on the sand near Point Conception listening to the waves lap the shore and watching the stars gradually appear in a reluctantly darkening sky. I was thinking about this remarkable region, this Southland as its newspapers like to call it, whose sustained magnetism is unmatched in history. Southern California's population boom began in the 1870's, and its residents have been increasing dramatically in number ever since. For all of that time it has shown an astonishing ability to attract visitors, to attract new citizens, in general to attract attention.

Why?

There is no simple answer, of course. At the root is an appeal tied to comfort, aesthetics, and adventure: a generally benign climate combined with handsome, exciting physical geography, permitting a wide range of activities within a short span of time and distance. And there is the obvious economic attraction of natural wealth, from fertile farmlands to a generous ocean to deep pools of oil.

Beyond that, southern California for a century has been glamorized and publicized by the sellers of real estate, of transportation, of movie tickets. No wonder the world's attention was riveted and its imagination aroused.

But in recent decades, through the popular media, that vast audience has been given, I suspect, more slanted information about southern California than has ever been generated about any other place.

My own observations are personal and limited, but not necessarily superficial. I have been visiting this area, sometimes for extended periods, for nearly half a century. Because I know something about it, I am often taken aback by the impressions held by people I meet in other parts of the country and of the world who have visited here only fleetingly or have been dependent on what they could learn from writers, broadcasters, or filmmakers.

What people typically hear about are the extremes. Not surprisingly, it is these extremes—trend, fad, cliché; the bizarre, the outrageous; exaggeration or exploitation—that seem to make up by far the greater part of the world's picture of southern California. The extremes exist; they come and go, persist or disappear; but they are not the essence of this society, any more than Atlantic City or Wall Street represents the essence of life on the Eastern Seaboard.

All along this southern California coast are men, women, boys, and girls who eat and sleep, work and play, study and sweat, and aspire and strike out just like their contemporaries in the rest of the United States. Perhaps they have more fun: They don't have to shovel snow, and the sun shines much of the time, and the beaches and the mountains are close by. But they still have to find jobs and pass examinations and get along with each other, and most of them face and meet these challenges day by day pretty much the way their cousins do in Pennsylvania or Illinois or Montana. They are the vast majority of the people who populate southern California; and they are not cultists or addicts or dropouts.

Two of them—cheerful teenagers strolling the beach in the deepening dusk—interrupted my musing to warn me that the tide was coming in. As I started the long hike back to my car, a cool wind was rising, a reminder that Point Conception marks the edge of California's balmy southern province. I looked again at the ranch lights scattered along the channel coast, then turned my steps and my thoughts northward.

Designers, inventors, filmmakers, partners—Charles and Ray Eames enjoy a rare occasion: Sunday morning together in their home near Santa Monica. The couple built the house, "a pleasant place for living and working," in 1949. He died in 1978 after living more than half his 71 years in California. He once said, "Just being by an ocean is comforting."

Twilight mist and spray brighten sea-washed rocks in the Big Sur country. In the distance, Bixby Creek Bridge spans a challenging gorge; longest of 33 bridges in a 73-mile stretch of the coast highway, it provides overlooks for a world-famous shore.

Cruising northward above the Golden Gate Bridge, a seaplane offers its occupants an unobstructed view of downtown San Francisco and the harbor. The city covers the tip of a peninsula that juts between the 450-square-mile bay and the Pacific.

Their fleece set aglow by late-afternoon sun, sheep graze above the Bear River; fog caps the headland of Cape Mendocino, westernmost point in California. To the south, the King Range rises from the shoreline, forcing roads to run miles inland.

Ranches—many encompassing 5,000 acres or more—cover much of this remote country. Timber harvesting supplements income from livestock and crops. Farther up the coast, logging becomes the predominant industry.

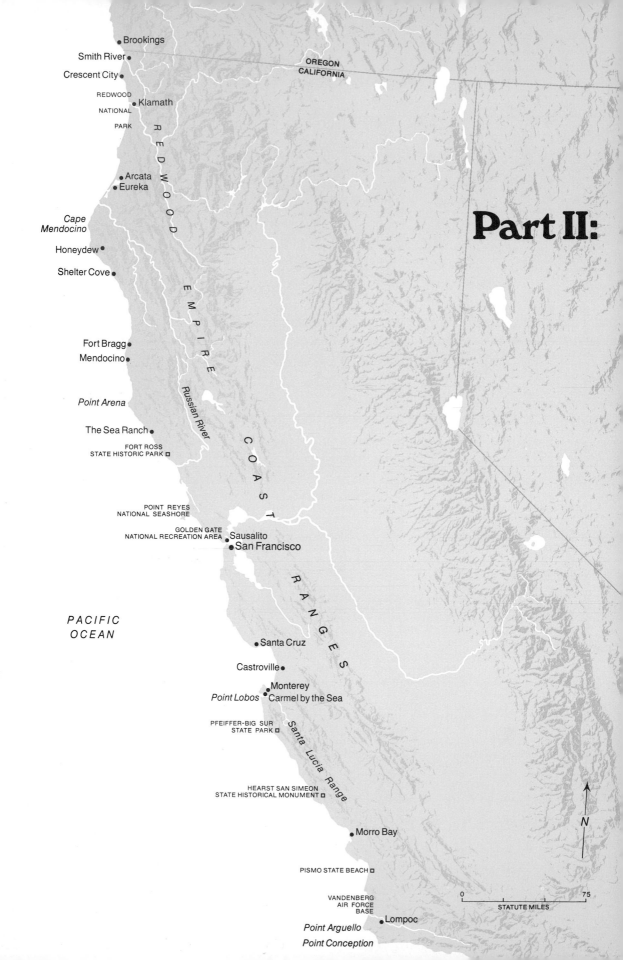

Part II:

Brookings
Smith River
Crescent City
OREGON
CALIFORNIA
REDWOOD
Klamath
NATIONAL
PARK

Arcata
Eureka

Cape
Mendocino

Honeydew
Shelter Cove

Fort Bragg
Mendocino

Point Arena

The Sea Ranch
FORT ROSS
STATE HISTORIC PARK

POINT REYES
NATIONAL SEASHORE
GOLDEN GATE
NATIONAL RECREATION AREA
Sausalito
San Francisco

PACIFIC
OCEAN

Santa Cruz

Castroville

Monterey
Point Lobos
Carmel by the Sea

PFEIFFER-BIG SUR
STATE PARK

HEARST SAN SIMEON
STATE HISTORICAL MONUMENT

Morro Bay

PISMO STATE BEACH

VANDENBERG
AIR FORCE
BASE

Point Arguello

Point Conception

Lompoc

REDWOOD EMPIRE COAST RANGES

Russian River

Santa Lucia Range

N

0   75
STATUTE MILES

Central and Northern California

TO THE PRESENT-DAY OBSERVER, with access to accurate maps and airplane windows, San Francisco Bay is by far the most obvious feature of the northern California coast. Yet the narrowness of its Golden Gate and the prevalence of fog seem to have kept it hidden from seafarers for the first 226 years of the white man's occasional reconnaissance in these parts. The bay's discovery was left to a small party of Spanish soldiers who came upon it by land. To them it was primarily an obstacle; and even after the establishment of a presidio and mission on the peninsula's tip, the splendid harbor was assigned little importance until the great California gold rush.

On his deathbed at San Miguel island in January 1543, Captain Cabrillo had asked his men to continue their difficult expedition. Under the Levantine pilot Bartolomé Ferrelo they did so. Some historians believe they paralleled the full length of the California coast before turning back. Yet they missed all the significant harbors along their way, and received little credit when they finally arrived, exhausted and ill, back at Navidad on the west coast of Mexico. It was 59 years before the authorities of New Spain bothered to dispatch another ship specifically to explore Alta California, although galleons returning to Acapulco from Manila sailed down the coast periodically, and the crews of some of them made tentative forays ashore.

In the meantime an Englishman, Francis Drake, and the crew of his privateer *Golden Hind* became the second group of Europeans to visit the California coast. On his way around the world, the intrepid Drake needed to pause and repair his ship. In the summer of 1579 he spent five weeks in a protected harbor somewhere in the vicinity of San Francisco Bay; but his brief account permits us only to speculate on whether he actually entered the bay itself.

In 1602-03 the adventurer Sebastian Vizcaíno explored the northern coast, naming Monterey Bay for the Spanish viceroy and later describing it as having a far better harbor than the bay actually affords. Yet even this glowing and misleading report did little to stimulate further Spanish interest for another 166 years. "The lapse . . . emphasizes the utter isolation of

Most of the coastal population of central and northern California clusters around
such bayside cities as Monterey, Santa Cruz, San Francisco, and Eureka.
The rest of this part of the Sunset Coast remains mostly rural, the home of ranchers
and lumberjacks, fishermen and poets. Scenic highways make much
of it accessible to motorists; memorable drives wind along the stone ramparts
of the Big Sur country and through the ancient groves of Redwood National Park.

California and the low regard in which the Spaniards held it," writes historian Walton E. Bean. "California was a place that should have contained gold, but apparently did not; a place where a strait should have been, but was not; a barren and dangerous coast that a ship sailed past once a year. Getting to it from Mexico was far more trouble than it was worth." So it was not until 1769 that Father Serra and Captain Portolá began the long, hard task of establishing the missions and presidios of a Spanish colonial period that ended with Mexican independence in 1821.

California's much-romanticized quarter-century as a territory of Mexico was marked by rapid expansion of trade with New England merchants eager to buy the hides produced on the great ranchos. There was contact, too, with the Russians, who ruled Alaska and, unchallenged, had planted a colony at Fort Ross, only 65 miles north of the Golden Gate. Then the United States and Mexico went to war; and by the Treaty of Guadalupe Hidalgo, signed in February 1848, California was part of a vast area ceded to the United States. At that moment—more than three centuries after Spain had first laid claim to this remote land—there were only about 15,000 non-Indians in all of California.

But by a fascinating and ironic accident of timing, the end of the war coincided almost exactly with the most significant event in California's history: discovery of gold in the foothills of the Sierra Nevada. In 1850 California was admitted to the Union, and by 1852 the new state counted a population of nearly 224,000. Five years before, the village of Yerba Buena had claimed perhaps a hundred residents. Renamed San Francisco, and fatefully located to serve as the principal gateway to the gold fields, it had become by 1852 a boisterous city of 35,000.

Today, of course, the bay is the hub of a thriving nine-county metropolitan area. Oakland and Richmond—on the east bay shore—as well as San Francisco are major ports; Oakland and San Jose are large and lively cities, and Berkeley is a key name in academic circles. But San Francisco continues in its dominant role. With a personality that springs partly from its physical setting and partly from a century and a third of colorful history, it seems secure as one of the most admired of American cities.

Certainly it is a place that leaves indelible memories. It caters to all the senses in distinctive ways: the view from a distance of its white houses climbing the hills, or the curve of mist-haloed lights on the bridges late at night; the aroma of a sourdough bakery or of a dew-dampened eucalyptus grove; the feel underfoot of a wooden wharf or a stone-paved walk; the sound of a foghorn or a cable-car bell, or the sweet, clear notes of Taps floating down from the Presidio.

Anyone who has been to San Francisco has his own list.

THE URBAN COMPLEX of the bay area, however, is not typical of the central and northern California coast, most of which forms a striking contrast with populous southern California.

Because U. S. Highway 101 turns inland near Gaviota, most of the travelers who see the quiet, cattle-grazed hillsides sloping to Point Conception are riders on Amtrak's *Coast Starlight*. The Southern Pacific tracks stay close to the ocean, angling northwest at Government Point and tracing the edge of high bluffs south of Jalama.

From a boundary five miles north of the lighthouse at Point Conception, Vandenberg Air Force Base with its restricted space-rocket and test-missile launch sites occupies nearly 35 miles of the shore. Then several small resort towns—of which the best known are Pismo Beach and Morro Bay—

*Moderating ocean currents and prevailing westerly winds
contribute to the even climate of the California coast.
Fog and rainfall increase as the shoreline reaches northward;
vegetation of the coastal slopes gradually changes
from chaparral and scattered oaks to dense conifer forests.
But the pattern of dry summers holds almost to the Oregon
border. Active fault zones and rugged mountains testify
to the region's turbulent geologic past.*

mark the approach to the still sparsely populated Big Sur country, a ruggedly scenic coastline fronting the Santa Lucia Range and reaching from San Simeon almost to Carmel by the Sea.

Big Sur takes its name from that of the Big Sur River, a half-anglicized corruption of the Spanish *Rio Grande del Sur,* big river of the south.

Towns crowd the coast again from the Monterey Peninsula to Santa Cruz. But the western slopes of the coastal hills approaching San Francisco are still almost unpopulated. From the Golden Gate north, the only coastal cities larger than 7,000 people are Eureka and Arcata, on Humboldt Bay.

Thus, although the southern California coast is now mostly urban, the state's central and northern shoreline is still essentially rural. How long this will continue to be true is one of the principal questions facing Californians. How much development should be permitted along those parts of the coast that remain in their natural or nearly natural state?

In an effort to guide such development and to "preserve, protect, and where possible, to restore the resources of the coastal zone," the voters in 1972 adopted a California Coastal Initiative that called for a long-term plan to address those objectives. The plan has been prepared and adopted, and the Legislature and the California Coastal Commission are now considering some of the problems it has helped bring into focus.

THE COASTAL CLIMATE of California north of Point Conception is distinguished from that to the south chiefly by the orientation of the land and by colder ocean temperatures. Whereas the shore from San Diego to Point Conception curves generally northwest, with many beaches facing south or southwest, the coastline from here on aims much more steadily northwest to north. So it is more exposed to the influences of the North Pacific, and has more wind and fog. Still, air temperatures are moderate, and the rainfall pattern—dry summers and relatively wet winters—continues almost to Oregon. Only in Del Norte County, in California's northwest corner, is there a pattern of occasional summer rains.

It is in this cool, foggy climate that the rare and inspiring coast redwoods make their appearance. They grow in a belt little more than 30 miles wide extending northward from Monterey County. They are the world's tallest trees, and they have given coastal northern California its nickname: the Redwood Empire.

"The mountains push close to the sea"

"T MINUS TEN AND HOLDING," came the metallic voice from a public-address speaker outside the briefing room. The young Air Force captain interrupted his talk to visiting observers and listened.

"Not another scrubbed mission!" I thought, hoping intently for better luck than Jim Sugar had experienced earlier here at Vandenberg Air Force Base. Jim had positioned his camera to photograph a fire-breathing missile rising against the background of a full moon. But the huge silo door had jammed, and the launch had been canceled.

The loudspeaker delivered another announcement, and the captain expanded on it: "There's a satellite passing over," he said. "I don't know whether it's American or Soviet, or the reason for holding—whether it's because we might hit it, or because it might pick up some data that"—he paused delicately—"that perhaps it should not."

He continued his briefing, and soon a recurring *beep* signaled that the countdown had resumed. A few minutes later we moved outside and up the hillside to wait for the launch.

Because our position was masked from the launch site by an intervening ridge, the first evidence of ignition was a brightening glow above the ridgeline. Then an elongated fireball appeared, rising steeply on its skyward course: a speeding Minuteman III intercontinental ballistic missile, invisible in the dark except for its brilliant flaming tail.

During its 5,000-mile journey, it would reach an altitude of 700 miles before curving down to land—in less than 25 minutes—near Kwajalein Atoll in the Marshall Islands.

The spectacle did not end with the launch. In the vanishing fireball's path far above us a curious afterglow appeared, an eerie fluorescent effect as white-hot particles of residual solid fuel diffused in a great cloud, then very slowly faded.

It was a memorable climax to my visit to one of the nation's largest aerospace installations. At 98,400 acres, Vandenberg is exceeded in size only by John F. Kennedy among space centers, and by Eglin and Edwards among Air Force bases. Jutting into the Pacific at Point Arguello, it can launch over water through a full 180 degrees of the compass. As headquarters of the Western Test Range, it carries out missions for the National Aeronautics and Space Administration, the Navy, and private industry as well as the Air Force.

Most of the work of Vandenberg, however, is related to its role as the principal training and testing center for the Air Force's missilemen. Earlier that day I had watched some of the intensive training, aided by *(Continued on page 115)*

(Continued on page 115)

Water like molten sunset thunders into a tunnel of wave-sculptured sandstone along the wild, craggy Big Sur shore. On this stretch of open coast, rocks take the full fury of the sea—often with results as spectacular as this.

WILLIAM L. ALLEN, NATIONAL GEOGRAPHIC STAFF

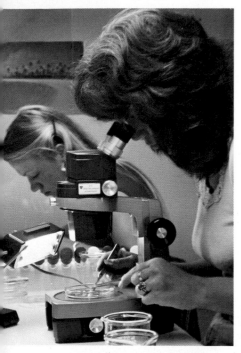

Nasturtiums splash the Lompoc Valley with color in late July. By August, the W. Atlee Burpee Co. will harvest the seeds, using the old farm buildings for storage. Wholesale seed companies prize the valley's fertile soil and cool coastal climate, planting 2,000 acres of flowers each season. At Sandyland

Nursery in Carpinteria, a different method of production prevails; it replaces the old practice of rooting sizable cuttings. Instead, technicians dissect buds (left). Then test-tube batches of tissue receive nutrients and hormones, developing rapidly as rotating racks control exposure to artificial light. By this process Sandyland can market many thousands of plants a week. Such sophisticated nursery technology has helped make California the nation's largest producer of ornamental plants.

Ready for firing, an unarmed Minuteman II intercontinental missile waits in its silo at Vandenberg Air Force Base, the only U. S. military installation that test-launches such weapons. At upper left, the combat crew commander, First Lt. Joseph L. Dorris, monitors a control panel during preparation for the countdown. In the "job control room," visual display boards log each step prior to launch. Miles away on the 98,400-acre base, gantries stand unused, ghostly relics of the early missile program.

Tires churning, a dune buggy charges up a hundred-foot slope at Pismo
State Beach. Tracks show where other drivers turned and circled back near the
top. On a long holiday weekend, more than 4,000 off-road vehicles swarm
across the 850-acre area set aside for their use. Amateur racers like Jim Pitts
(left) compete in a variety of informal hill climbs and other events. A Pismo
veteran, he steers a handmade buggy powered by a Corvair engine. In a more
orthodox vehicle, a dog waits for its owner to return.

FOLLOWING PAGES: Time-exposure photography creates a tracery of light as
a driver stops to watch a nighttime race. Serious about their play, some
Californians spend as much as $10,000 on a dune buggy.

89

Dream castles by the sea: Hereford cattle roam grassland beneath towers of the famed estate that once belonged to newspaper magnate William Randolph Hearst. Zebras and other exotic animals also graze the fields around La Cuesta Encantada, the Enchanted Hill. At right, a tour group pauses in the dining hall to gaze at a 16th-century ceiling taken from an Italian monastery. Hearst spent millions of dollars on art for the place once described as his "shrine of beauty." Seven miles away in Cambria Pines, 84-year-old Art Beal—also known as Captain Nitwit and Dr. Tinkerpaw—has worked 50 years creating a castle from castoffs. The structure, recognized by the State as a place "worthy of preservation," descends a 250-foot cliff. Beal turned his dream into reality with scrap lumber and auto parts, abalone shells and beer cans. Outside, a sign reads: "Caution—Adults at Play."

Piedras Blancas Lighthouse, 90 miles north of Point Conception, warns ships of perilous shallows. Along the area's gently shelving strands, tide pools hold a rich variety of life. Twice monthly, tides fall below normal levels, attracting a flurry of feeding gulls—and studious marine biologists. Dr. Eric Hochberg holds a two-spot octopus, one of many creatures that reach the northern limit of their range near Point Conception.

95

Intellectuals and artists value the seclusion of the Big Sur country. In the study of his oceanside home, Linus Pauling—the world's only recipient of two unshared Nobel Prizes—pursues interests ranging from the structure of metals to the benefits of vitamin C. "I think that there will always remain something to be discovered," he says. Above, Ansel Adams stands before one of his famous photographs of Yosemite National Park; this large print of the face of Half Dome, taken in spring snow in 1927, hangs in his living room. Best known for his sensitive landscapes, he takes pride in other work, including portraits. He believes in "intuitive expression controlled by exacting technique."

PRECEDING PAGES: Morning fog clings to the steep slopes of the Santa Lucia Range.

Jagged islands off Point Lobos rise from a sea made golden by afternoon sunlight. Storm waves as high as 35 feet sometimes batter these granite crests, on calmer days the favorite roosts of cormorants and gulls. Spanish explorers, daring the coastal waters in the 18th century, used the term lobos marinos, or "sea wolves," for the sea lions that frequent the rocks. Point Lobos became a state marine reserve in 1960. For decades the region inspired Robinson Jeffers, once characterized by a fellow writer as the poet of an American wilderness "dangerously close to sundown." He often came here "To feel and speak the astonishing beauty of things—earth, stone and water. . . ."

Craggy inlets and tricky winds force golfers into risky drives from the tees on the 16th and 17th holes of the Cypress Point Club at Pebble Beach. Touring pros consider the course one of the most challenging in the country. Below, a wave plumes against abandoned buildings of Monterey's Cannery Row, made famous in 1945 by John Steinbeck's novel. Twenty-three canneries employed more than 5,000 people until the late 1940's, when sardines almost disappeared from coastal waters. Above, a picker empties a canvas backpack of artichokes into a storage bin near Castroville, self-proclaimed Artichoke Center of the World. Cool ocean winds and moist summer fog produce ideal growing conditions in the Monterey Bay area, which yields the bulk of the nation's artichoke crop.

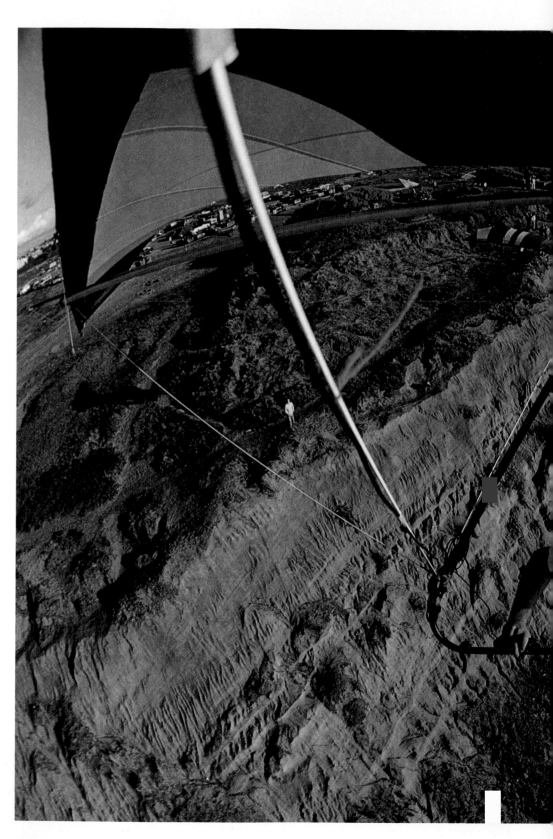

High over cliff and sea, hang gliders ride the onshore wind at Fort Funston, in San Francisco. Pilot Gary William Koehler flies his Seagull Ten Meter northward to join friends.

Sustained winds between 12 and 20 miles an hour let advanced pilots stay aloft for hours and return to takeoff points atop the cliffs, avoiding the long climb up from the beach.

Fog rolls in from the ocean almost daily during San Francisco's summer months. As a thick bank engulfs commuters on the Golden Gate Bridge, the city's skyline still glimmers in the sun. Long-time residents can track the fog's approach by the distinctive sounds of fog signals around the bay. Below, morning mist hangs over the city's Noe Valley.

With firm strokes, members of the
Dolphin Swimming and Boating Club—all but
one over 60—plow through cold waters off
Fisherman's Wharf. Founded in 1877, the club
sponsors hazardous swims around Alcatraz and
under the Golden Gate Bridge. The Coast Guard
requires fluorescent orange caps that boatmen can
see at a distance. Above right, longshoreman-
philosopher Eric Hoffer, a highly acclaimed
author, muses in his spartan apartment. After
a career on the docks, he says: "I have no talents
greater than the people I have lived with." In
nearby North Beach, Mario Crismani and his son
Paolo welcome the regulars at the Bohemian Cigar
Store, known for its special cappuccino.
PRECEDING PAGES: A wide-angle lens captures
much of San Francisco's financial district and the
revitalized Embarcadero area. A helicopter float,
a safety feature for overwater flights, appears
sharply curved at upper left and right.

Star of the line, gripman Carl A. Payne entertains cable-car passengers with quips and rhythmic chimes on the car's bell, also rung as a warning at intersections. In 1978 he won San Francisco's annual Cable Car Bell Ringing Contest the second year in

a row for the best original composition by a gripman. The lever in his hands sets the
car in motion by closing a grip on a steel cable that runs at a steady nine miles an hour
through a slot between the tracks. Track and wheel brakes help control the car, with
yet another brake for emergencies. Working the Hyde Street Line, Payne ends his hilly run at
Aquatic Park—where tourists leaving the cable car may well encounter the Automatic
Human Jukebox. The more favorable the reaction of the "machine" to the patron,
the better the "jukebox" will play, both offbeat and old-time attractions.

computers and simulators, that prepares new officers to operate the control centers of the nation's 1,054 deployed Minuteman and Titan missiles. Periodically, to test the condition of the weapons themselves as well as the proficiency of the crews, a missile is selected at random, pulled out of its hole in North Dakota or elsewhere, and brought to Vandenberg for a test firing. It was such a launch I had just observed.

As it turned out, all went well that night despite the delay, and when I left Vandenberg everyone was in good spirits. But less than a month later, tragedy struck the base—ironically, not from a malfunction of any of the complex missile systems with which its people routinely deal, but from a 10,000-acre chaparral fire that swept over the dry hills, trapping and killing the base commander, fire chief, and assistant chief.

Because of the nature of Vandenberg's mission, the strands and bluffs of its 35-mile coastline are closed to the public. But the base is flanked by recreational beaches—a county park at Jalama, just to the south, and a state beach at Point Sal, on the north. Fifteen miles farther north, Pismo State Beach offers an expanse of coastal dunes and long, level stretches of sand that are the habitat of the famed Pismo clam.

ABOUT HALFWAY between nearby Avila Beach and Morro Bay is one of the most controversial of the nation's power-generating projects, Pacific Gas and Electric Company's Diablo Canyon Nuclear Power Plant. Flying a light plane along the coast one bright spring day, I looked down on the construction site. Between a small cove and the Irish Hills, amid the marks of massive earth-moving, rose a long, rectangular building backed by tall twin white domes. Near the plant's main structure were smaller buildings, roads, and the beginnings of a transmission network.

Later I learned that the plant, scheduled for completion by the end of 1978, contains two nuclear units that will have a combined capacity of 2,190,000 kilowatts, increasing the company's generating capability by 20 percent.

Although the Diablo Canyon site was accepted by some conservationists as an alternative to a scenic dunes area farther south, other environmentalists have opposed it from the beginning—and still hope to block the issuance of its operating permit. Their ranks swelled with the discovery of a geological fault offshore that runs within a few miles of the plant. Thereafter the design was modified to provide for additional potential earthquake stress.

One opposing group, the Abalone Alliance, has taken a threefold stand. Its members are morally opposed to nuclear power. They object to this plant, in what was an undeveloped section of the coast, on environmental and ecological grounds. And they oppose the specific location because of the unpredictable earthquake factor.

When I asked representatives of PG&E and the Abalone Alliance for summaries of their positions, I was provided with a generous supply of material. As I studied the issue, I became increasingly frustrated; for the two sides repeatedly offered as facts totally conflicting statements.

For example, on safety:

From PG&E: "In all the years nuclear reactors have been operated by electric utilities in the U. S., no property damage or injury to the public or operating personnel has ever been caused by radiation from these facilities."

From the Abalone Alliance: "Nuclear power plants routinely release invisible poisonous radiation into the air and water. . . . [and] the frequent abnormal operations and accidents at nuclear plants

One of the "bus people" around Santa Cruz celebrates the day from the door of her home—a repainted and refurbished school bus. When police move in to enforce camping regulations, these beach squatters must move on. California attracts new residents of all ages who dream of a youthful freedom, an easy and unhassled life.

release much larger amounts of radiation than are normally released."

On generation of nuclear wastes:

From PG&E: "A single 1,000,000-kilowatt nuclear plant generates only about two cubic yards of high-level waste per year."

From the Alliance: ". . . 10-18 shipments per year of this [highly radioactive] waste will be hauled by truck to the Pismo Beach railroad siding. . . ."

On the cost of nuclear power:

From PG&E: ". . . nuclear power is the cleanest, cheapest source of 'heat energy' today—and probably for the next several decades. . . ."

From the Alliance: "Nuclear electricity is more expensive than electricity from coal plants nearly everywhere. . . ."

And so it went. There were comparable contradictions on the questions of nuclear plant reliability, thermal effects on nearby ocean water, and so on. No wonder conscientious laymen trying to arrive at a responsible position on the subject of nuclear power are bewildered.

Morro Bay's distinctive trademark, though it must compete with the stacks of a huge steam power plant, is massive Morro Rock, rearing 576 feet at the entrance to the harbor. A fishing port and water resort, Morro Bay is the last town of any real size on the drive north toward the rugged Big Sur country. But before the mountains push close to the sea, there is a stretch of about 40 miles in which the shoreline eases up gradually toward rolling hills, and broad, sloping pastures are edged by streams and occasional stands of oaks or eucalyptus. In this peaceful setting, near San Simeon, rises the castle that was once the estate of publisher William Randolph Hearst.

Long before the present buildings were assembled, when this was simply a rustic vacation spot, the young Hearst wrote an evocative description of the area: "I love this place. . . . I love the sea and I love the mountains and the hollows in the hills and the shady places in the creeks and the fine old oaks, and even the hot bushy hillsides—full of quail—and the canyons full of deer."

When he inherited the property in 1919, Hearst began the construction that was to continue on an ever grander scale until 1947, four years before his death. What eventually emerged was a trio of lavish guest houses in Mediterranean style, enhanced by gardens, fountains, and pools and surmounted by the twin-towered La Casa Grande. The entire complex, from the great halls to the small sitting rooms, was constructed and furnished with materials of rare craftsmanship and objects of art collected throughout the world.

It was an astonishing tour de force. And to enable the public to share the result, the Hearst Corporation deeded the property to the State of California in the late 1950's. After 20 years it is still a heavily visited attraction.

Over several visits I have spent hours wandering the buildings and grounds, yet I realize I have hardly begun to sort it all out. Even so, I think my favorite recollections of it are the views, from an elevated but relatively close vantage, provided by light plane or helicopter. As the craft circles, La Cuesta Encantada—the Enchanted Hill—appears to turn like some elegant model castle displayed on a revolving stage. Its palms and cypresses, chimneys and spires, tile and water surfaces form a rich pattern of color and light and shadow. Somehow, held thus at arm's length, it seems more comprehensible.

ON THIS QUIET Big Sur coast, overlooking Salmon Creek north of Cambria and San Simeon, Linus Pauling and his wife, Ava, spend as much time as he is willing to take at age 77 from an active professional life.

An independent and sometimes controversial figure in both science and politics, Pauling is twice a Nobel laureate, winner of the award in chemistry in 1954 and of the peace prize for 1962. Yet a stranger might never suspect the toughness of fiber underneath the kindly, cheerful exterior.

Jim Sugar visited the Paulings at Salmon Creek and describes the experience this way: "The Paulings' house—one of those wonderful, sprawling rock, redwood, and glass contemporary structures—sits at the end of a long, winding dirt road near the base of a steep hill. During a storm the waves and ocean spray must lash the house; but on this winter day the sea was calm, the sky blue, and the sun so warm we were able to sit on the large deck, drinking tea and enjoying the view.

"When I arrived, Mrs. Pauling was writing a letter in German to a friend in Europe, and Dr. Pauling was reading the draft of a research monograph. They were in 'at-home' clothes, and Dr. Pauling was wearing a jaunty beret.

"Both of them are very unpretentious. But all about them—the walls of books, paintings and posters, a grand piano—were indications of the intellectual intensity of this family. Pauling's desk was piled with papers. Several molecular models rested atop the bookshelves, and on a wall of the study were two posters in Russian announcing his lectures before a Soviet scientific group.

"I photographed for more than an hour, but he never became impatient."

When I met Dr. Pauling later in Menlo Park, at the Linus Pauling Institute of Science and Medicine, the dress and surroundings were more formal but the manner no less gracious. Very tall, his ruddy face glowing with good health, he is a walking advertisement for generous daily dosages of the vitamin C in which he has such confidence.

Although his current research involves many other aspects of preventive medicine, it was vitamin C in particular and nutrition therapy in general that we talked about. For I was interested that it has taken Dr. Pauling years to get the medical profession to pay much attention to his reports, despite remarkable results he and a Scottish colleague have obtained by administering massive amounts of vitamin C to cancer patients considered terminally ill.

"I know there's interest, finally," he said, "though it's hard to get details. Doctors don't like to talk about their patients, and still aren't ready to publish. But, for example, some Stanford people are now using vitamin C. And at last we seem to be getting some response from the National Cancer Institute."

North of San Simeon begins what seems to me one of the loneliest stretches of the entire California coast. It is 70 winding, cliffside miles to the Big Sur River, which lends its name to this section of the Santa Lucia Range. Here State Highway 1, famous for its scenery, offers some of its most outstanding views. It is frustrating to be the driver when the land, the sea, and perhaps a sunset keep enticing your eyes from a narrow and unpredictable road a thousand feet above the water.

South of Pfeiffer-Big Sur State Park the coast redwoods first appear, southernmost in a range that extends into Oregon. Beyond the park is the promontory of Point Lobos, which with its tumbled, tilted rocks and gnarled Monterey cypresses has been called "the grandest meeting of land and water in the world." Here is a prime place to watch furry sea otters as they play tag or roll in the water on their backs, rocking with the waves and cracking shellfish against rocks balanced on their chests.

One route linking Carmel by the Sea and Pacific Grove is the Seventeen-Mile Drive, well known both for its seascapes and for the treacherous golf courses it skirts. But the heart of the Monterey Peninsula is Monterey itself, a town of color and contrasts, of historic buildings and busy waterfront, of echoes of such famous residents as Robert Louis Stevenson and John Steinbeck.

Much has changed, of course, including the street Steinbeck brought to life in *Cannery Row*. In the late 1940's the sardine population off Monterey all but disappeared, and the packing plants that lined Cannery Row closed down. Some of the sagging old buildings are still there, and the street has several shops and restaurants catering to tourists, but it is no longer the vibrant little world of Steinbeck's stories.

At least one passage in *Cannery Row* still applies, however. Rise soon enough and this is what you will find:

"Early morning is a time of magic in Cannery Row. In the gray time after the light has come and before the sun has risen, the Row seems to hang suspended out of time in a silvery light. The street lights go out, and the weeds are a brilliant green. The corrugated iron of the canneries glows with the pearly lucence of platinum or old pewter. No automobiles are running then. The street is silent of progress and business. And the rush and drag of the waves can be heard as they splash in among the piles of the canneries. It is a time of great peace, a deserted time, a little era of rest."

Elsewhere the Monterey Peninsula is still one of the liveliest places on the entire Pacific Coast, with a seemingly endless schedule of special events: Bach festivals and jazz festivals, golf tournaments and car races, rodeos and fairs, art shows and house tours, and all of a scale or quality to draw throngs from out of town. It is a poor place to look for a hotel room late on a weekend evening.

Monterey Bay curves past the big Army training center at Fort Ord, past Castroville and Watsonville, to Santa Cruz, northern California's most popular beach resort. Though Castroville is the smallest of these communities, it has the most imposing title—Artichoke Center of the World. Here, on a few square miles of fertile ground shaded and cooled by frequent fog, grows almost all of the commercial artichoke production of the United States.

For years Nat Bracco has been managing 700 acres of artichoke fields for Sea Mist Farms. A courteous, articulate man, he explained to me the growth cycle of the big, shaggy, thistle-like plants and their happy adaptation to the climate of Monterey Bay.

"In the wild, in their native habitat—the Iberian and North African coasts—they're accustomed to hot, dry summers and cool, wet winters. There, winter is when they put on most of their growth," he said. "Here the frequent fog or overcast convinces them it is winter all the time—so we can grow them year round. We get close to 12 months' harvest, with some ups and downs.

"We set out cuttings in late spring and well into summer. We stagger the planting schedule to prolong production, and the dry months are a good time to get them started. Irrigation, when it's needed, is almost 100 percent by sprinkler. The work is pretty well mechanized except for harvesting, which still requires hand-picking."

I asked whether he had to take on extra workers at certain seasons. "This is a fairly labor-intensive crop," he said, "but it's one of the most even throughout the year in its requirements. So most of our workers are here all the time."

Pickers collect the artichokes in canvas backpacks, then transfer them to large bins on tractor trailers to be hauled to the packing shed. There they are sorted and graded, chilled in ice water, and packed for shipment.

I had noticed a Sea Mist field that was marked as a research plot. "That's an industry-sponsored project conducted by the Department of Agriculture; we provided the land," Nat said. "We hope to develop improved varieties, learn better cultural methods, and increase resistance to our worst pest, the plume moth larva."

The artichoke fields of Castroville, the begonia gardens of Capitola, the redwood groves north of Santa Cruz—mile by mile northern California's microclimates change the scene. On the bay side of the mountains approaching the San Francisco Peninsula the urban strip begins at Los Gatos, but on the ocean side the drive remains pleasantly rural beside wooded hillsides, along the San Mateo County beaches, and past the farms and fisheries of Half Moon Bay. Then the coastline steepens, so that you have almost reached San Francisco before suburbia becomes apparent.

San Francisco! For a great variety of reasons, some more likely felt than thought out, it is a favorite city of countless Americans. But one reason, no doubt, is that it is *definable*. In an age of the formless, seemingly endless metropolis with no particular focus, San Francisco is a specific place, with visible limits, in a matchless setting. Its hills, its waterfront, its bay, its bridges, and—not the least—its cable cars all contribute to the city's distinctive personality. *And* its cable-car bell ringers!

Long ago an imaginative San Francisco gripman, yanking the cord that rang the clear, musical note of his car's warning bell, realized that with some practice he could play a sprightly rhythm. Soon he had challengers, and more and more gripmen began developing their personal styles of bell-ringing.

The cable cars make their way up the steep hills of the city by means of a moving cable that runs beneath the streets. Operating a lever called the grip, the gripman engages the cable when the car is ready to move, and releases it when he wishes to stop. He also operates a second lever and a foot pedal, both of which control brakes.

This requires strength and good reflexes, but it soon becomes second nature to a well-coordinated gripman, who then often has time and a free hand to rap out a one-tone tune on the bell.

For many years, San Francisco businessmen have been sponsoring a bell-ringing contest for the gripmen. I met the reigning champion, Carl Payne, one misty morning at the end of the Hyde Street Line when there was a temporary power reduction, so we had a few minutes to talk before the next run.

A native of Pittsburgh, Carl was discharged from the Marine Corps at Treasure Island, and liked the bay area enough that he decided to stay. After two years as a driver for the Municipal Railway, he transferred to cable cars in 1963 and has been a gripman ever since. For about ten years he has been entering the bell-ringing competition, and after placing third once and second several times, he won the top prize in 1977 and again in 1978.

"We have a lot of fun," he said. "The guys like it, and there are some good prizes, donated by the merchants."

Early each summer an elimination contest is conducted at the car house. "Everyone enters who wants to, and the elimination usually takes about two days," Carl said. "Then the judges pick six finalists, and they compete in Union Square about a week later. That's open to the public, and the mayor and other officials are there. They have a motorized cable car they can drive into the square. It's quite a big event."

Successful bell-ringing is all in the wrist, the champion explained. And with that—the power having been restored—the car filled with passengers, conductor Sel Colon stepped aboard, and we were off. The bell rang out a merry beat that cleared the intersections and caused smiling heads to turn as we rolled up and over Russian Hill, past the edge of Chinatown, over Nob Hill, and down to Powell and Market.

SAN FRANCISCO is a city of parks, thanks largely to John McLaren. The durable Scotsman served as the city's park superintendent for almost 56 years—until his death in 1943 at the age of 96. And in addition to the system he developed, crowned by the creation of 1,017-acre Golden Gate Park from arid, shifting dunes, the Army's parklike Presidio of San Francisco has added another prominent greenbelt of grass, trees, and ornamental plants to the cityscape.

But by far the most remarkable recent parks-and-recreation development on the Pacific Coast has been establishment of the Golden Gate National Recreation Area. It was an impressive political achievement, because it involved cooperation and agreement not only by numerous local, state, and federal agencies but also by San Francisco voters. It has brought together dozens of elements—extensive military reservations as well as city, state, and federal parks—under the unified management of the National Park Service.

The result is a consolidated coastal park that runs almost without interruption from Fort Funston on the south, along the ocean beaches and bay waterfront to Aquatic Park; includes Alcatraz and Angel islands in the bay; and resumes on the Marin headlands across the Golden Gate, to extend northward to the Point Reyes National Seashore.

The achievement is so new and so unusual that the community is still analyzing the possibilities it unfolds. A proposed management plan will be submitted for general review and public hearings in 1979. Whatever final plan emerges will evolve slowly and carefully. "Nowhere else in the country do so many people live in such close range of a national park with such a variety of resources," says one of the preliminary studies. "One hundred thousand acres of coastal open space . . . containing representative examples of seashores, forests, estuaries, and marine environments of the North Pacific Coast . . . adjacent to a metropolitan population of five million is a precious combination."

John McLaren, it seems to me, would be proud.

From Eric Hoffer's 17th-floor apartment you can see parts of the new coastal park; closer at hand are the docks where Hoffer worked for nearly 30 years. Author of eight books—including *The True Believer* and *Reflections on the Human Condition*—this writer-laborer is surely one of the most unassuming of philosophers. At one point in our conversation he expressed his admiration for longshoreman leader Harry Bridges, and I asked if he had known Bridges personally.

"No! Never spoke to him," he replied emphatically. "I am *not* a man of affairs. I am as common as common can be. You couldn't tell me from any other longshoreman on the waterfront."

Although he lives in an elegant building with an expansive view, Hoffer's quarters are as simple as the man himself. The furnishings are a narrow bed, two or three chairs, a desk and bookshelves, and a record player. On the small balcony beyond the window, a single plant bore one bright flower.

In his rich, deep voice, with an accent influenced both by his Alsatian parents and by the German woman who took care of him after his mother's death, Hoffer told about his childhood in the Bronx. At the age of 7, he lost his sight as the result of a fall, and was blind until he was 15, when his sight spontaneously returned. "But in retrospect," he said, "that was a wonderful time.

Martha Bauer was a remarkable woman, and she *really* loved me, she *really* took care of me." He leaned into certain words with a rolling stress. "She absolutely dedicated her life to me. We talked about everything under the sun, and later she would recall what I had said. Imagine that! She made me think everything I said was worth remembering. She gave me confidence. You know, a man's confidence is basically the confidence a woman has in him."

Hoffer's father died soon after the boy regained his sight, and at 18 he went west, arriving in southern California with $300 and a wicker basket full of books. When the money was gone and the books were sold, he started picking up odd jobs and "learning the ropes."

"That was when I began to know this country," he said. "And despite being poor, and hearing all the agitators talk—in 1921 there was a small depression—I fell in love with America. I sensed that this is the only country for me. I'd tell everybody: For us common people, this is our Fatherland. This is our last chance, our last stop. If we don't make it here, we won't make it anywhere else.

"It's still true. There's still opportunity here for anyone who *really* makes an effort, who doesn't just sit and wait for something to drop into his lap."

Hoffer worked in Los Angeles until the Great Depression; then he went on the road. "Ah, that was my time of prosperity," he said. "It took very little money to live, and I had a wonderful time. I worked on construction jobs, in lumber camps, in the orchards picking fruit. I met some marvelous people."

When did he first go to work on the waterfront?

"When the war broke out. Do you know, they wouldn't take me in the Army because I had a hernia! So I went to work on the docks, lifting heavy loads all day." His hearty laugh echoed across the room.

It was just after the war that he started to write. "The first book took two years—I remember I started it during the three-month strike of 1946 and finished it during the three-month strike of '48," he said. "It was an enormous effort for me. Then I spent 1949 rewriting it. I submitted it in longhand—I didn't even know it was supposed to be typed. But they accepted it."

We walked toward the door, still talking. "I do very little writing now," he said. "You know, old age is the real thing; it's not a rumor. And what you need most when you are old is somebody who loves you. That is something you can't provide. You need the grace of God—to find yourself in your late 70's with people you love dearly and who love you. And I have that." With a strong handshake, he wished me well.

"IT'S THE LAST manned light station on the Pacific Coast," Herk Schuber said. "It's also one of the oldest lighthouses still in use on this coast. And incidentally, it's the only one in the United States, I'm told, that's reached by a suspension bridge."

As second in command of the Coast Guard's Point Bonita Light Station, Machinery Technician Second Class Schuber was in charge on the sunny September day of my visit. Everyone understood this except Lance, a rambunctious young Doberman pinscher with a marked tendency toward insubordination. With Herk, Lance, and Coast Guardsman George Thomas, I set out on the ten-minute walk to the light from the station's main cluster of buildings. Herk answered my questions between fierce commands aimed at Lance as the dog dashed off in one direction, then another to investigate the brushy hillside.

The path wound through the dry chaparral, much of the time affording a clear view back across the Golden Gate to the shining white skyline of San Francisco. Finally we made our way through a tunnel and across the footbridge to the sheer tip of the rocky point. There, its cylindrical lantern room offset above a larger building, stood the venerable lighthouse.

"The first light was built in 1855 up on the hill, where the radar is now," Herk said. "But it wasn't a satisfactory site—too high above the fog—so in 1857 they moved it here, with the lantern about 130 feet above the water. The year before, the West Coast's first sound signal was installed; it was a cannon fired every 30 minutes when the fog was in."

Today a foghorn can be turned on from the station headquarters, and the light operates automatically. "But we still pull duty at the lighthouse because, for the time being at least, it's a key weather-watching post for the entrance to San Francisco Bay," Herk said.

Nevertheless, the days of this last manned light station apparently are numbered. Sometime in 1979 the Coast Guard expects to have in place the intricate electronic equipment that will enable Point Bonita to go to fully automated status.

"Most of the time, things are pretty dull," Herk said. "But when there's a storm, this can be an exciting place. We get drenching spray from the waves up here, even though the control room is 115 feet above the sea."

As we climbed about the solid old structure, George Thomas showed me the beautiful Fresnel lens that magnifies a 1,000-watt bulb—or, for that matter, a kerosene lamp, as in past years—into a beam rated at a million candlepower and visible 18 miles at sea.

On the way back, I was struck again by the contrast between the city just across the Golden Gate and the quiet, natural scene around us. As if to reinforce the point, Lance flushed a yearling doe from the brush. With a shout Herk brought the dog to heel, then watched the deer bound down the steep hillside, leap gracefully over a streambed, and disappear from view.

"Windswept, grassy hills and murmuring forests"

UNTIL RECENTLY the Marin headlands opposite San Francisco were military reservations mostly off limits to the public. Today, as part of the new Golden Gate National Recreation Area, they mark the threshold of a coastal strip of parkland that extends northward more than 40 miles, encompassing the moody redwood groves of Muir Woods, the crest of Mount Tamalpais, the long spit of Stinson Beach, and Point Reyes National Seashore.

This is the province of fishermen and swimmers, tide-poolers and rockhounds, and especially of hikers. The heights of Tamalpais permit long views out over the bay area; and the windswept, grassy hills and murmuring forests of the Point Reyes Peninsula offer a hundred-mile network of trails. Here the slopes have long been pastureland for dairymen, and herds still graze where private rights have been reserved within the park. On damp, chill days, chimney smoke rises above the steep roofs of comfortable old farmhouses to mingle with wisps of low-hanging clouds in the folds of the hills.

A curved hook at the end of the peninsula completes the arc of Drake's Bay. Some scholars believe an inlet in this bay is the sheltering cove described by Francis Drake in 1579 on his voyage around the world. Discovery 40 years ago near San Quentin of an inscribed brass plate seemed to shift the evidence to favor a corner of San Francisco Bay as Drake's refuge. But in 1977, new techniques of analysis indicated that the plate is of fairly recent vintage. If so, it is one of the cleverest and most convincing hoaxes ever undertaken. At this point, both authorship of the plate and the location of Drake's wintering place remain intriguing puzzles.

North of long, slender Tomales Bay, which traces the line of the famed San Andreas Fault, Highway 1 wanders back toward the ocean; and from Bodega Bay to Rockport, for more than a hundred miles of the Sonoma and Mendocino coasts, it is again a scenic route mostly faithful to the shoreline. To be sure, this is far gentler terrain than the rugged cliffs or offshore rocks to north and south. Sloping hills, studded in places with outcroppings of gray rock, angle toward the sea. After a wet winter the land is carpeted with thick green turf embroidered with perky yellow buttercups, white daisies, and long-stemmed lavender lupine. Windbreaks of cypress and scattered groves of sycamores, oaks, and pines combine with grazing sheep and rustic fences to provide endless inspiration for Sunday painters.

At Jenner the Russian River, known for its steelhead trout fishing, comes sweeping out of the coastal mountains. But in the *(Continued on page 139)*

On a headland notorious for wind and fog, Point Reyes Lighthouse beams its warning. Nearby, the San Andreas Fault, flooded by the sea, divides the peninsula from the mainland. Sea, terrain, and weather ally to give the northern California coast its secluded majesty.

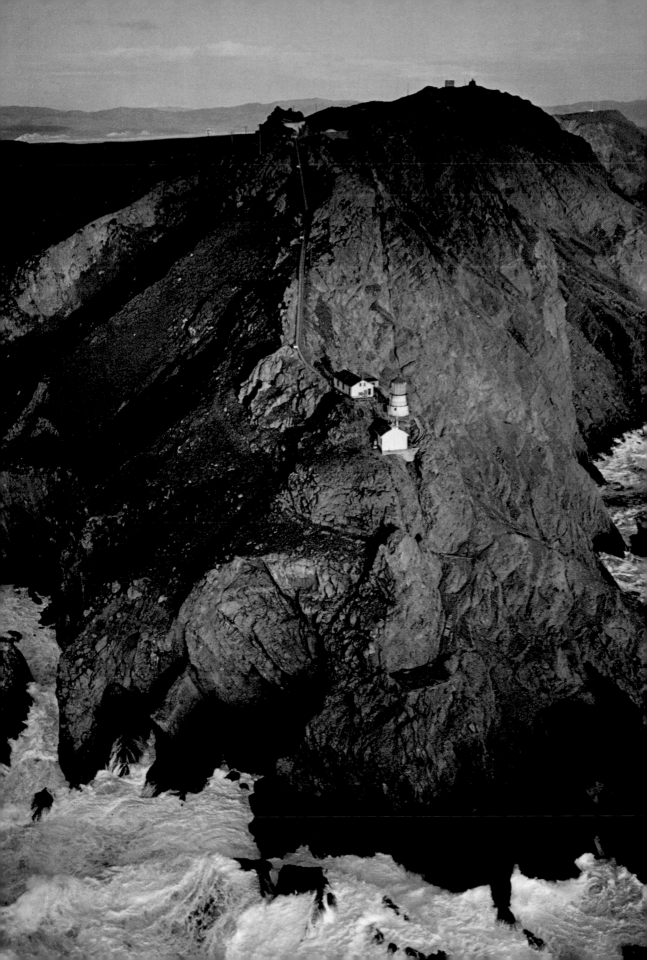

124

Remnant of a houseboat community labeled
"Bohemia afloat," Phantasmagoria lies off Sausalito in
Richardson Bay. A relaxed policy on marina conditions
attracted scores of houseboats to the bay in the
1960's. Now, Marin County officials enforce more
stringent standards. At a renovated pier Steve and
Nancy Frisch relax aboard Green Dragon. "Our roof
gives the illusion of space," she says, "but it
leaks a lot." Ashore, fabric artist Jeri Brittell
stitches one of her many quilts portraying the
California coast. Her works hang in collectors' homes
and art galleries within the region and beyond.

Artists lured to a tranquil but vivid setting bring vitality to Mendocino, once a bustling lumber town. Painter Dorr Bothwell finds it "inspirational." The Gloriana Opera Company thrives as one of two theater groups; here singers apply makeup for The Mikado. *A young resident of a nearby Christian commune, The Lord's Land, puffs at a dandelion near a homemade water tank on a huge redwood stump.*

Stalwart sentry of another day, William Owens, 77, renews an old acquaintanceship with Point Cabrillo Light Station (left). Here Owens served the final 11 of his 33 years as a lighthouse keeper; he recalls waves battering the foundation in a 1960 storm. His friend Jim O'Donnell (right), now a spry 89, saw the lamp installed in 1908. Curved prisms of its Fresnel lens concentrate light rays into a single beam with 1.3 million candlepower. Coast Guardsman Herk Schuber utilizes a rainy day to clean the lantern room at Point Bonita Light Station, one of several marking the entrance to San Francisco Bay. For more than a century ships under sail or steam depended on manned lighthouses and fog signals to mark safe channels or warn of danger. Today automation takes over.

"Anything automatic always goes haywire just when you need it," says Owens; "we'll have a big wreck one of these days." But in 1978, except at Point Bonita, the coast's automated sentinels kept their vigil alone.

Mounted hired man, assisted by herd dogs, rounds up ewes and lambs for inoculations and tail-docking at Ocean View Ranch near Cape Mendocino. This fertile land yields luxuriant grass for livestock. About 40 ranches here run both sheep and cattle. Lambs, usually born in January, go to market in June. The hilly Cape Mendocino area remains primarily open pastureland, beyond the reach—so far—of intense development. In the tiny town of Honeydew, Rusty, a Brittany spaniel, keeps a sharp eye out for customers. Not counting summer travelers, fifty or sixty patrons a day stop at the general-store-and-post-office that constitutes "downtown" Honeydew. Residents must drive 50 miles north to Fortuna to the nearest movie theater; most high-school students board with families in Ferndale, 45 miles to the north. Store owner Joy Branstetter grew up in Honeydew, married the boy next door, and reared six children. "I've never been tempted to leave," she says.

Burnished jewel of Victoriana, this 19th-century mansion in Eureka endures as one of the finest examples of Victorian house-building in the West. Its 18 rooms, each rich in texture, color, and detail, display eight varieties of wood. Intricately carved primavera, a Central American hardwood, embellishes the entrance hall and grand staircase. Medieval figures in stained glass adorn the doors. Music, one of the four arts depicted in stained-glass windows, gazes wistfully down the stairs. The exterior, mostly carved from redwood, incorporates a tower, balconies, gables, pilasters, and columns in unabashed devotion to the Victorian creed that the more ornamentation, the better.

Choker setter Brenda Benoit loops a steel cable—a choker—around a redwood log so a yarder rig can drag it away for removal by truck. If a felled tree leaves no room beneath it for securing the cable, she uses explosives to blast out working space. For five years one of the few female choker setters on the Pacific Coast, she explains, "I don't like to work indoors." Not many well-paying jobs for women exist in the northern California coastal area, she says. "We're proud folk up here. We bust our tails for what we get, and we don't want any handouts." Humboldt and Del Norte counties produce most of California's commercial redwood. Controversy simmers, and sometimes flares, over the local logging industry. Critics argue that cutting speeds erosion, endangering streams and vegetation— including protected trees. Others emphasize that logging provides jobs in a region afflicted with high unemployment, and further stress that trees constitute a renewable resource.

After work, Brenda horses around with fellow loggers at Butch's Club in Klamath. "They accept me," she says, "because I do my job."

December mist surrounds a
bull elk, member of the resident
herd of Roosevelt elk in Prairie
Creek Redwoods State Park. The
male loses his antlers in late
winter. A new set starts to grow
in spring as the cows that made
up his harem during the mating
season begin dropping calves.
A big bull stands five feet at the
shoulders and weighs 800 to
900 pounds; he can sprint at
some 35 miles an hour.
Officials remind everyone: "The
elk are wild, so observe them
from a distance." Prairie Creek
and two other state parks lie
within the boundaries of
Redwood National Park,
established in 1968. Visitors
find excellent salmon and trout
fishing, good birdwatching, and
the chance of spotting whales
offshore in migration season.

spring of 1978 I found the town quiet. Heavy rains had swollen the river, making the banks inaccessible, and the fishing was the poorest in years.

A dozen miles northwest of Jenner, seemingly quite out of place and time, stand the restored remains of Russia's southernmost 19th-century settlement in North America. Fort Ross State Historic Park preserves the reconstructed stockade and two buildings of a Russian colony that occupied this site from 1812 to 1841, hunting sea otters, farming, and trading with communities of Spanish and Mexican California.

The park's retired historian, John C. McKenzie, and his wife, Alice, live nearby and spend much of their free time on the grounds as volunteers for the Fort Ross Interpretive Association as well as the park. Their knowledge of the site and its history enlivened my tour of the commandant's house and the chapel. As I was leaving, they advised me to look sharply into the small cove as I walked up the hill to my car. When I did, I spied more than a dozen harbor seals bobbing lazily in the protected waters.

A**T SEVERAL POINTS** along the Sonoma and Mendocino coasts are striking concentrations of contemporary residential architecture. The largest and in some ways most innovative is The Sea Ranch, which stretches for ten miles along a still nearly wild shoreline. The developers have described their site and objective in simple and evocative terms: "Ocean bluff or meadow, grassy slope or forest. . . . a spectacular stretch of coastal land, and a visionary plan: Unobtrusive homes of natural materials, loosely clustered around large common areas to preserve open space, views, natural flora and fauna." The results have won several architectural and planning awards.

North of Point Arena, the open sweep of the land becomes more tightly organized. The road winds among pastures, cultivated fields, and long windbreaks, and there are more farmhouses and villages, giving the countryside an almost European appearance.

At Little River I visited a veteran of 33 years—actually 32 years, 11 months, and 19 days—with the old Light House Service and, after consolidation, the Coast Guard. His name is Bill Owens, and he and his wife, Isabel, were stationed for 11 of those years at nearby Point Cabrillo and for 15 at Point Arena. A crusty, emphatic Kentuckian who regularly punctuates his conversation with phrases like "those screwball politicians in Washington," Owens declared that automation of such navigational aids as lighthouses was one of the worst things the screwballs had ever done.

"Anything automatic always goes haywire just when you need it," he said. "Besides, those old lighthouse keepers saved a lot of lives. Flesh and blood can do something in an emergency. What can a bell buoy do? You can't even hear the bell in a bad storm."

Owens has an endless supply of yarns from his long service in an uncommon occupation. Some have happy endings, some sad, some ironic.

"On December 11, 1941," he said, "a Japanese submarine surfaced just opposite the lighthouse at Point Arena. I watched it for several minutes while two men stuck their heads out of the hatch and looked around in every direction. Then they resubmerged.

"Of course, I reported it immediately to naval intelligence. And they wouldn't believe me. It couldn't have been a Japanese sub, they said. Impossible.

"That very night a Japanese submarine sank a lumber schooner just north of Fort Bragg. Put a torpedo right

A tired-out pooch, a willing pony, and an adventurous young man pause to rest beside the coast highway. Bud Kenny of Bismarck, Arkansas, with his dog Muscoda and pony Maybelline, trekked across America in search of the nation's character. During three months in northern California, he found "a lot of isolation, friendly people, and plenty of room. Someday, I'll make it my home."

through the engine room. Only a few of the crew were saved.

"The next day, here came a little parade of naval officers. All this brass coming down to see a boatswain's mate. They swore me to secrecy about the sub sighting for the duration of the war. I suppose they're all admirals now!"

Once a dedicated sportfisherman, Bill had to give that up after a stroke in 1973. But his interest in life and enthusiasm for his "clan" is unabated. "Isabel and I have six daughters—all raised on a light station—17 grandchildren, and 10 great-grandchildren. We like to gather on holidays, usually Thanksgiving and the Fourth of July. We have quite a time."

Bill Owens also maintains some long-standing friendships. One of them is with a man I particularly wanted to see because he was a survivor of the great California earthquake of 1906.

Then, as now, James H. O'Donnell lived in Mendocino, although he spent many of the intervening years in Oakland. At 89, Jim O'Donnell is—I am convinced—indestructible. When he was 64, after more than his normal share of hard knocks, he fell 40 feet from a highway bridge on which he was working as a carpenter and suffered multiple fractures. "I had over a hundred X rays," he told me. "I was an invalid for four years, but I stuck with the therapy and eventually recovered my health and went back to work. Different occupation, though— caretaker of some historic buildings. I didn't retire until 1975.

"You know, you have to make yourself go. I get plenty of fresh air and exercise. I still cut wood for the stove, but I don't get up in the trees to prune much any more. Well, I did have to top some not long ago.

"I had to stop dancing for a while after my cataract operation, but now I'm back at it. That's good exercise, too. I really like to dance—old-time dances, you know. I especially like Lawrence Welk's music."

O'Donnell has a vivid memory of April 18, 1906. "I was 17 years old and janitor of the high school, so I was up early cooking myself some breakfast," he said. "The stove began jumping around, and the coffeepot. I started to go outside, but the bricks were flying about, so I decided to stay put till it was over. I remember that the steeple snapped right off the Catholic Church. The big brick chimney collapsed at the mill; in fact, chimneys went down all over town. I worked all that summer vacation with bricklayers replacing people's chimneys.

"On your way out of town, look at the four houses just east of Mendosa's store," he said. "Those wooden houses were well built, well nailed. They were shaken right off their foundations and dropped about four feet to the ground, but they held together. Later they were raised up, new foundations were built— and they're still standing."

I did look. The four houses are doing just fine. Oh, yes, one other thing: New horizons are still opening for the durable Jim O'Donnell. Recently he was a great success in his little theater debut as Dr. Harper, the clergyman, in *Arsenic and Old Lace*.

I SPENT THAT NIGHT in surroundings reminiscent of an era even more distant than 1906. The town of Mendocino has retained its turn-of-the-century appearance, assured in recent years by the architectural controls of a county ordinance solicited by the town's residents. In 1975 the old Mendocino Hotel reopened after a thorough remodeling that combined modern comforts with the ambience of an elegant, small hostelry of the late Victorian period.

I took a room there, and slept soundly in a high four-poster bed. My clothes hung in a free-standing hardwood wardrobe. The room was finished in a wallpaper of baroque design that harmonized with the thick, rich red carpet. French windows opened out on a private balcony. In an immaculate bathroom across the hall, the efficiency of modern plumbing detracted not at all from the appeal of the old-fashioned light fixtures and gleaming tile surfaces.

Next morning, after a breakfast of

fresh fruit and three different home-made breads, I asked assistant manager Virginia Engleman how this pleasant anachronism came about.

"The owner is Robert Peterson, a San Diego businessman whose father was born in Mendocino," she said. "After the town was listed in the National Register of Historic Places, he had a chance to buy the old hotel. He decided it would be an enjoyable, worthwhile challenge to try to recapture the flavor of a fine, small-town hotel of that earlier time.

"There was extensive reconstruction of the interior. The furnishings came from other parts of the country as well as the West. They're a mixture of antiques—about 75 percent—and replicas.

"We have 26 rooms and a high occupancy rate, especially in summer and at holiday periods. Most of our clientele is from the San Francisco Bay area, but we get people from far and wide. And they're a nice mix of young and old."

At first glance Mendocino's neighbor, Fort Bragg, with its commercial strip along the highway and a huge, modern lumber mill, looks as typical of contemporary America as Mendocino looks like yesteryear. "But," said a long-time resident of the county, "a stranger will find his niche a lot sooner in Mendocino than here. This is a conservative, traditional place in almost every way: a kind of a company town, a close-knit community with well-established institutions, strong family ties, and great ethnic consciousness. We have lots of Finns, Italians, Portuguese from the Azores, Mexicans direct from Mexico.

"Unless you've lived here more than 35 years, you're considered a youngster or a newcomer. Our mayor recently retired after serving 21 years; he'd been on the council seven years before that. Fortunately, he was a good mayor.

"Don't misunderstand. It may take a long time to be fully accepted here, but the people are the kindest in the world."

Later I met Bernard J. Vaughn, the former mayor, who had weathered his 28 years of municipal politics without visible marks. He is a genial, scholarly man with wavy white hair who talks philosophically about some of the things he remembers. "There was more courtesy and trust in the old days," he said. "Lively debates, but a willingness to compromise. Then came all the revolt and disputation of the '60's, and the whole atmosphere changed. Still, everything considered, controversy made it more interesting. Anyway, I've never taken myself too seriously, and that helped. I enjoyed a good argument, and I tried to remember that I was a public servant."

Before leaving town I called on Andre and Arlene Schade, in their great museum of a house that contains five organs, three pianos, all kinds of unusual furniture and keepsakes, and unexpected nooks and crannies. The biggest surprise comes at the end of the tour. The third story is one large, splendid room, added by the original owner in 1897 to accommodate the churchless Baptist congregation to which he belonged, and entirely finished in hand-fitted, burnished redwood. The Schades call it the ballroom, and use it not only for entertaining but also as a family music center and library.

For 30 miles north of Fort Bragg I traversed coastal hills brightened by the yellow of Scotch broom and the lavender of lupine. In the early spring of 1978, however, it would have taken more than blossoms to offset the sodden sense of water, water everywhere: from overhead, incessant rain; to the west, the gray ocean; to the east, hilltops hidden by low clouds, valleys made mysterious by random fingers of fog. Water gushed down ditches and across the road, turned slopes into minor landslides, sprayed from the wheels of slicker-clad cyclists, and coursed off the rain gear of farmers and utility workers.

Then, a few miles north of Rockport, the coast highway turns inland to merge at Leggett with U. S. 101. That route finally returns to the coast at Eureka, but for the shoreline's intervening 80 miles the ocean can be reached at only a few points by spur roads, and only two of these are paved. One leads west from Garberville to Shelter Cove. The other makes a loop, leaving U. S. 101 at South Fork, passing through the hamlets of Honeydew and Petrolia to Cape Mendocino, California's westernmost point, then curling back through Ferndale to the highway at Fernbridge.

This loop drive is a delightful journey through redwood forest and rugged ranchland into an earlier California of infrequent crossroads stores, sturdy schoolhouses, and remote livestock corrals. North of Petrolia, named for a short-lived oil-drilling operation started soon after the 1849 gold rush, the road edges the shore for about five miles before turning inland at Cape Mendocino. Frequently—in the spring of the heavy rains—temporary signs cautioned "One-Lane Road Ahead." Translation: A chunk of the road has been washed away; or a landslide has partly blocked the pavement.

Right at the cape is the ranch of Joe Russ III and his wife, Annette. Cattle and sheep dot the green hills, and the ranch house—except that it has no neighbors—could be part of some well-spruced suburban scene: freshly painted and surrounded by flowerbeds, a newly mown lawn, and a trim white fence.

Looking at this picture-book setting, I thought: "I could be very happy here—except for the wind. I wonder if it ever stops blowing." Down the road, I paused to ask that question of a cowboy astride a big bay horse. "I don't know," he replied. "It hasn't yet."

I drove to Shelter Cove on another day of unsettled weather. The road climbs high over mountains of the King Range, which through much of this section of the coast shove their way close to the water. Ascending, I found myself in low-hanging clouds so thick I had to slow to five miles an hour. Suddenly, near the summit, I broke out into the bright sunshine. Spread before me was a great sweep of mountainside dropping to a broad, low point that protects a small cove just to the south.

Several resorts and a commercial fishing enterprise occupy the waterfront area. To the north extends a 13-year-old real-estate development, Shelter Cove Sea Park, with paved roads and utilities in place. The entire subdivision covers 2,640 acres, divided into 4,500 lots. About 50 retirement or vacation homes have been built, and another several hundred lots have been sold.

WITH A POPULATION of 25,000, Eureka is the largest California coastal city north of the San Francisco Bay area, and the hub of a busy complex that includes the university town of Arcata, the industrial town of Samoa, and the mills and docks on Humboldt Bay.

Historically and still primarily a lumber town, Eureka also derives significant income from fishing, tourism, and its growing importance as a seat of government agencies—federal and state as well as local. Higher education for the region is also centered nearby.

On a new site about eight miles south of Eureka stands the College of the Redwoods, one of California's extensive network of two-year community colleges. Buildings of native stone and redwood fit harmoniously into a sloping hillside backed by forests of spruce and fir. Offering both academic and technical courses, the college has pioneered vocational instruction in several fields. For example, it has a highly respected program in law enforcement—one of whose more colorful-sounding subjects is Control of Cattle Rustling.

At Arcata, seven miles north of Eureka, Humboldt State University carries on an academic tradition that began 65 years ago with the establishment of a state normal school. After several stages of evolution as a teachers college and liberal arts college, it is now a university comprising five schools and two divisions, with an enrollment of 7,500.

Eureka boasts a remarkable number of Victorian buildings in good condition, both within and outside its recently refurbished Old Town district. There several blocks of houses and business buildings have been repainted, and the whole scene enhanced by a landscape plan that emphasizes brick paving, gas lights, and new plantings.

My guide to much of Eureka, including Old Town and the port facilities, was Leslie M. Westfall, who first came to this part of the world as a young cavalry officer early in World War II. After overseas service he returned to stay, and today the Westfall Stevedore Company loads or unloads most of the ships that call at the Port of Eureka.

Although the port handles a large volume of cargo, there is a low-key atmosphere to the waterfront operations. Eleven docks are comfortably spaced along the shores of the bay, and there is none of the congestion of the big-city harbors to the south. Most outgoing vessels carry some form of forest products.

"The timber industry has changed a great deal," the tall, silver-haired Westfall said, "especially in the direction of consolidation and new technology. In 1952 there were about 400 sawmills in Humboldt County; now there are 31, some of course very large.

"And where we used to ship mostly finished lumber, now there's the whole range. Wood chips to Japan, wood pulp all over the world, logs to Japan and Korea, lumber and plywood to northern Europe and Mediterranean ports.

"There has also been a big reduction in the man-hours involved in longshore work in the last 25 years, because of mechanization and the changes in design of ships—use of containers, bulk handling of by-products like wood chips, and so forth.

"Selling what used to be waste material, such as wood chips and sawdust, now makes the difference in profit and loss for some of the timber companies."

We went aboard a Japanese cargo ship with a huge, empty hold. From a mountain of wood chips at dockside a conveyor-pipe reached to the ship's deck, where the loose chips were blown into the hold by compressed air. "Those will end up in a Japanese pulp mill," Les said. "A few years ago they would have been burned."

Citizens' complaints about intrusions of government are not uncommon anywhere in the United States today. But along the northern California coast, still in many ways a pioneer society of rugged individualists, two issues have stirred especially strong resentment. One was the adoption by California voters in 1972 of Proposition 20, an initiative measure to control future development of the state's coastline. The other was the establishment by Congress of the Redwood National Park in 1968 and its expansion in 1978.

Proposition 20 declared, "The permanent protection of the remaining natural and scenic resources of the coastal zone is a paramount concern to present and future residents of the State and nation."

To conservationists and, in general, public-spirited citizens in other parts of the state—including many in the southern two-thirds who had observed the results of unrestricted private ownership and commercial exploitation of the shoreline—the Coastal Initiative represented a better-late-than-never recognition of the fragile and irreplaceable qualities of the seacoast, and a commitment to careful planning for its future.

But to those who expected to be adversely affected—primarily owners and developers of real estate who might be told they could not do with their own property what they wanted to do—the impact of the new law ranged from annoying to infuriating.

The initiative established the California Coastal Zone Conservation Commission and six regional commissions. Their mandate was to administer the law, develop a comprehensive coastal plan, and, upon its adoption by the Legislature, implement its program.

In Eureka I talked with Rick Rayburn, executive director of the North Coast Regional Commission. "In the north coast counties—Del Norte, Humboldt, and Mendocino—an overwhelming majority voted against Proposition 20," he told me. "So you can imagine the emotion that has been generated. Actually, a high percentage of permit applications have been approved; but unpopular conditions have often been attached, things like density limits, protection of ocean views, public access, and preservation of wetlands. There's been a great deal of animosity—and real bitterness in cases of denial of permits.

"And, though there are only a few environmental groups, they keep a close eye on our actions."

But the controversies caused by the Coastal Initiative have been mild compared to those stirred up by the Redwood National Park acts of 1968 and 1978. The emotions involved are as basic as the rapture inspired by a stately grove of the world's tallest trees—or the angry frustration of a man who loses his job for reasons he considers unjustified.

Actually, government came quite late to the effort to set aside remnants of the matchless redwood forest that once covered two million acres of northern California and southern Oregon. In the laissez-faire days of the 19th and early 20th centuries, hundreds of thousands of the great trees were cut at a rate that within a few more decades would have eliminated the last of the giants.

In 1918, concerned citizens formed the Save-the-Redwoods League, and since then have bought hundreds of beautiful groves and donated them to the State of California for protection and enjoyment as public parks. Today the state system includes 21 redwood parks, and their preserves of virgin stands approximate 55,000 acres.

In the early 1960's there were still an estimated quarter of a million acres of unprotected virgin-growth redwoods. Yet, of the 106,000 acres brought under federal control by the two bitterly contested national park bills, only about 20,000 acres were old-growth trees. Perhaps another 50,000 acres survive in small, privately owned stands. The rest, logged while the political struggle wore on, are gone forever.

Most of the land authorized by the 1978 bill is a watershed buffer to ensure the protection of the park's more vulnerable trees. But because the legislation removed from commercial production 45,000 acres of timber-growing land, most residents of Del Norte and Humboldt counties were opposed to expansion of the park.

"I don't know anyone up here who objects to the idea of preserving choice virgin groves, within reason," Brenda Benoit said to me over a cup of strong black coffee. A slender but hardy young woman, Brenda a few hours earlier had been deep in the woods east of Klamath making her living as a logger.

"We love the state parks. They're well run, there are good facilities so the public can enjoy them, and we're proud of them. But then the Federal Government came in and took thousands of acres more, and in ten years they haven't done anything to make those areas accessible to anyone except backpackers. And now they're getting twice as much, most of it not even old growth. They're taking away our livelihood. The expansion bill was only passed a couple of months ago, and already I know of three sawmills that have closed."

Brenda's friend, Jerry Mistretta, joined in. "One of the ways they got the bill passed was by including retraining and reemployment provisions. But what about a 50-year-old man who's the best timber-faller around, well paid, and suddenly there's no more trees to fell? What are you going to retrain him to do? How do you know there'll even be a job in his new trade? So you end up offering him $2.50 an hour to pick up papers in the park."

The conversation turned to Brenda's unusual role. "She's among the few women I've heard of on a logging crew," said Jerry. "She's a choker setter—doing one of the toughest, most dangerous jobs in the woods. But she's got guts, and she's good at it."

The faller fells the tree. The bucker cuts it into sawmill lengths ranging from 18 to 40 feet. Then the choker setter wraps a steel cable, or choker, around the log—blasting a working space underneath with powder or dynamite if necessary—and secures the cable so it can be winched up the slope to be loaded on a truck.

Brenda answered the obvious question. "I wanted to work outdoors. And I wanted the money. Anyway, I love it— I like the challenge."

I learned of another challenge accepted by a young woman long ago when I called on Evelina Peine a few miles north of Klamath. Miss Peine was one of the first women in Del Norte County—"maybe even the first"—to attend the University of California, enrolling at Berkeley in 1917 to earn her teaching credentials.

A tiny, alert woman of 79, Miss Peine still lives on her dairy farm, now managed for her by a neighbor, Frank Karwaski. "She's got a heart bigger than she is," he told me. "You'd never know it from anything she says, but she's the most generous person I've ever known. She's helped so many people!"

Dressed in old clothes and rubber boots, surrounded by worn furniture and piles of newspapers—"I'm not much of a housekeeper, as you can see"—Miss Peine immediately put me at ease with the warmth of her welcome and her vivid reminiscences. Sitting straight as an arrow, her eyes bright, she recalled her years as a schoolteacher at Crescent City. "Oh, how I enjoyed teaching," she said. "I liked to help the children. They were my friends."

She also has affectionate memories of her parents, though they're "mostly memories of everyone working. We all worked so hard. They were both from Switzerland, but they met over here. We moved down from Crescent City in a horse-drawn wagon when I was two. This was wilderness then, all hills and hollows, with little meandering streams and lots of trees. Father cleared and leveled the ground for these meadows.

"He would get up at half past three to bring in the cows, and of course they all had to be milked by hand. It used to take 12 hours to haul a wagonload of potatoes to Crescent City. We'd follow the beach, while the tide was out.

"After teaching in town for several years, I came back here and taught at the country school about a mile away. That way I could help with the farm, too. And I've been here ever since. Gradually the roads came, the bridge, the town. I've seen it all."

Eventually, she saw the emergence of today's U. S. 101 as the builders worked their way past the farm. To the north, although the highway stays quite close to the Del Norte coast, the hills and tall trees screen out the ocean view most of the time. Here the coastline is largely forest-topped cliffs. When the road descends briefly, there are glimpses of offshore rocks; when it climbs, it yields occasional views out to sea. But it is the thick, straight, soaring redwood trees, veiled in fog or brightly patterned in sun, that stamp this land with their beauty and strength.

Then the highway descends in a long, sweeping curve toward the crescent-shaped bay for which the county's only incorporated town is named. A pleasant, quiet place with a spacious waterfront park, Crescent City still remembers one night of its past more vividly than all others.

The March 1964 earthquake that leveled Anchorage, Alaska, sent a great tidal wave coursing southeast, and Crescent City was in position to catch its full fury. The assault actually came in four waves, each hurling logs and debris, the fourth and last cresting at 20.78 feet above the mean low tide. Before the nightmare was over, 11 persons had died, nearly 300 houses and stores had been swept off their foundations or otherwise damaged, automobiles had been tossed about and battered into junk, and five large petroleum tanks had exploded and burned.

BUT NORMALLY Crescent City is almost as tranquil as the Smith River valley just to the north. Here the fertile fields produce about 12 million Easter lily bulbs a year, almost the entire supply for the United States. Among the major growers are Olaf Samuelsen and his son David. At their farm I talked about this specialized crop with Olaf's sister-in-law, Edna, and her daughter, Barbara Yoshioka.

"The wet, temperate climate and well-drained soil of these two counties, Del Norte in California and Curry in Oregon, are just right for lilies," Barbara said. "Typically the bulbs are grown over a three-year cycle. Bulblets taken from two- or three-year-old bulbs are set out in early fall. A year later they're dug, washed, treated, and replanted. The third year they're harvested.

"The normal blooming period here is July, but we usually pinch off the buds to increase bulb growth. We do let some bloom for our 'Easter in July' festival.

"About mid-October the harvested bulbs are shipped to cold-storage facilities and held until time to send them to greenhouses. There, bloom is forced for Easter."

"There's a lot of work involved," said Edna Samuelsen, who has been growing lily bulbs for 43 years.

"But you quickly come to love the lilies. And when they bloom out—oh, my, you can find your way home in the dark by their fragrance."

THE ECHO of Edna Samuelsen's words has come back to me more than once since that morning. Her feeling for the lilies, and for her home and her way of life, seems to typify something about the people of California's northern coast.

Not one man or woman I talked with wanted to move anywhere else. Many had lived elsewhere; their reasons for settling here were diverse, but obviously did not include a stereotyped preconception of California that specified palm trees, sunbathing beaches, and the facilities and entertainment of a big city. Nor were they drawn here by the promise of prosperity. The north coast counties chronically have an unemployment rate that is markedly higher than the national average.

In short, life is not easy here. The cool, foggy climate is not severe, but it can be difficult and depressing. Jobs are in short supply, and in places many amenities are lacking.

Yet there is a kind of pioneer enthusiasm, a frontier optimism of openness and cooperation. And there is also a willingness to work hard, combined with the recognition that there are other rewards in life beyond material gain. One of these rewards—some people obviously feel—is to be able to live where there is an abundance of natural beauty, clean air, and elbow room.

So these north coast Californians may be here because they like to hunt and fish; or because they like to watch the unfolding drama of a winter storm; or because their hearts are lifted every morning by the redwoods; or just because there are not too many people around. Or perhaps because it smells so good when the lilies are in bloom.

Beyond the town of Smith River the highway swings west toward the sea, crossing broad, green meadows. In their midst stands the studio of Oscar W. Johnston, sculptor and refugee from an engineering career in urban southern California. His art takes many forms, but I was particularly drawn to his deft renderings of north coast birds. These range from meticulously detailed decoys to whimsical, stylized shorebirds in steel-brushed, richly grained redwood.

In his wide-windowed house set among fields on the Pacific flyway, Oscar Johnston is in the right place to observe firsthand many of the birds he carves. Getting into my car, I looked up; overhead swept a flight of geese, headed north. I was going that way, myself. I waved goodbye and followed.

Fog cascades through a forest of coast redwoods, world's tallest trees. Once widespread in the Northern Hemisphere, they now grow only in California and the southwestern corner of Oregon—in a strip of land by the Pacific some 450 miles long and 30 miles wide.

Working in early mist near Coos Bay, Oregon, a lone "pond man" guides logs to a

sawmill. Rough-sawn there, they go then to a planer for smoothing into finished lumber.

PRECEDING PAGES: *Driving through erupting foam, a 44-foot Coast Guard lifeboat runs the breakers at the mouth of the Columbia River, chosen for training missions because of its extreme dangers. Coast Guardsmen based at nearby Cape Disappointment saved 40 lives in 1977 alone—and assisted hundreds in distress.*

Sea stacks, hewn from the mainland by the force of storms and shaped by erosion, resist wind and turbulent surf off Point of Arches, just beyond Olympic National Park in Washington. As a rule, erosion works slowly; but when great waves compress air into crannied rock, the sea can break off immense slabs of stone.

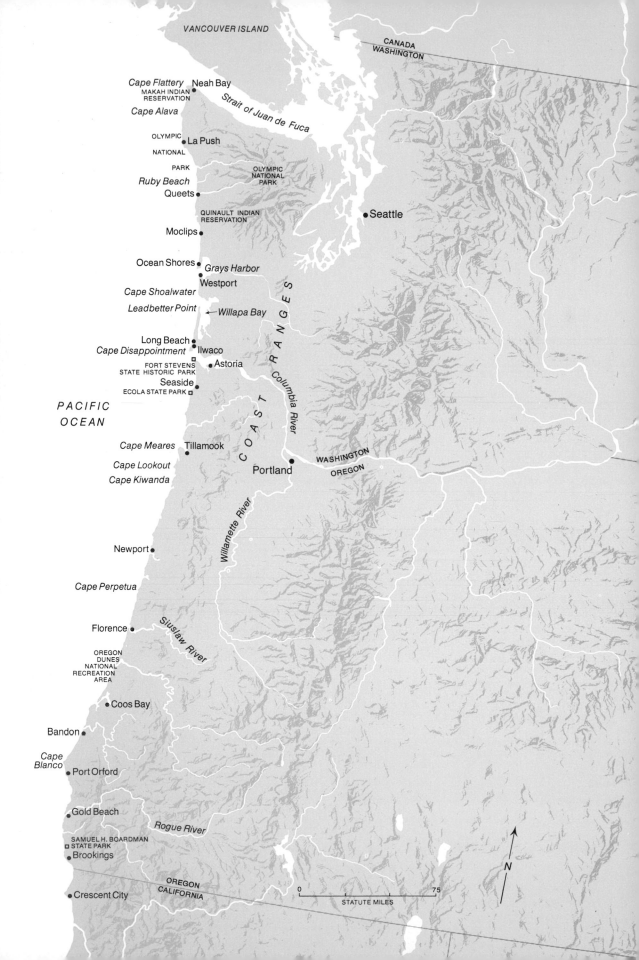

VANCOUVER ISLAND

CANADA
WASHINGTON

Cape Flattery • Neah Bay
MAKAH INDIAN
RESERVATION

Cape Alava

Strait of Juan de Fuca

OLYMPIC • La Push

NATIONAL

PARK

OLYMPIC
NATIONAL
PARK

Ruby Beach
Queets •

QUINAULT INDIAN
RESERVATION

• Seattle

Moclips •

Ocean Shores •
Grays Harbor
• Westport

Cape Shoalwater

Leadbetter Point ← *Willapa Bay*

*PACIFIC
OCEAN*

Long Beach •
Cape Disappointment • Ilwaco
FORT STEVENS □
STATE HISTORIC PARK
• Astoria

Seaside •
ECOLA STATE PARK □

Columbia River

C
O
A
S
T

R
A
N
G
E
S

Cape Meares • Tillamook

Cape Lookout

Cape Kiwanda

Portland •

WASHINGTON
OREGON

Willamette River

Newport •

Cape Perpetua

Siuslaw River

Florence •

OREGON
DUNES
NATIONAL
RECREATION
AREA

• Coos Bay

Bandon •

*Cape
Blanco*
• Port Orford

• Gold Beach

Rogue River

SAMUEL H. BOARDMAN
□ STATE PARK
• Brookings

OREGON
CALIFORNIA

0   75
STATUTE MILES

N

• Crescent City

Part III: The Pacific Northwest

THE LAST CONTINENTAL COASTLINE in the world to reveal itself in detail to inquisitive explorers—except for the polar regions—was the ocean edge of our Pacific Northwest. Such distant shores as those of Australia, Siberia, and a thousand far-flung islands were well known and carefully charted before the American Robert Gray sailed into the broad mouth of the Columbia River in 1792. Only five years before, Charles William Barkley of England had finally confirmed the location of the long-rumored Strait of Juan de Fuca.

Before Barkley, less than two dozen ships had made their way to the Oregon country over a period of two and a half centuries—and their skillful but preoccupied captains had done little in the way of mapping the coast. The fact that none of those experienced seamen had discovered and investigated the most prominent breaks in the northern shoreline underscores the difficulty they faced in navigating this region under sail: the contest with prevailing winds, the necessity of staying well away from a treacherously rocky shore, and the frequency of fog, rain, or low clouds that limited visibility.

The first Europeans known to have probed this far north were men already identified with early California history: Drake, in 1579; and Vizcaíno and his lieutenant, Martín d'Aguilar, in 1603. After that, the northern coast was ignored until the last third of the 18th century. Then a rekindled interest in a legendary Northwest Passage that was thought to link the Atlantic and Pacific across North America led to a new wave of exploration.

The Spanish, concerned about England's expanding maritime adventures and Russia's activity along the coast of Alaska, were anxious to control any such passage, and sent out three expeditions from Mexico in the years from 1774 to 1779. But none found the long-sought waterway, and two ships' crews were decimated by hostile Indians.

Meanwhile, the Englishman James Cook had made two long voyages into the southern and central Pacific that had greatly contributed to geographical knowledge. In 1776 he set out again, rounding the Cape of Good Hope and crossing the South Seas to arrive at last at New Albion—Drake's name for these lands—at about the 43rd parallel.

On the long northwestern shore, scattered communities manifest a range of life-styles. Coos Bay prospers as the center of Oregon's forest-products industry. Neah Bay in Washington serves as a fisherman's harbor—and as the capital of the Makah Indian Reservation. Crops of soil and sea reflect the varied resources of the coast—as distinctive as the cranberries grown near Bandon, the oysters harvested at Willapa Bay.   155

During the month of March 1778, Cook sailed up the coast of present-day Oregon and Washington. Eventually he sighted what "appeared to be a small opening, which flattered us with the hopes of finding an harbour." But low ground blocked the way, and—perhaps in a moment of whimsy—he named the prominent point of land just to the north Cape Flattery. Today the cape is the northwesternmost tip of the State of Washington and, by the definitions of this book, the northern end of America's Sunset Coast.

Somehow Captain Cook failed to see or recognize, beyond Cape Flattery, the wide opening to the Strait of Juan de Fuca—as he had already missed the mouth of the Columbia. He continued to the western shore of Vancouver Island, carefully scouted the edges of Alaska, entered the Arctic Ocean, then turned south for the islands of Hawaii, one of his earlier discoveries. There he met his death in a dispute with natives.

Cook's ships eventually made their way to China and on home to England. While in a Chinese port, the men learned how highly valued were the furs they had acquired from the coastal Indians—and that knowledge signaled a new era for the Pacific Northwest.

Just as the discovery of troves of silver and gold had fixed the attention of Spanish conquistadors on Mexico and Peru, so the promise of profits from furs suddenly made the Northwest of great interest to merchants of England and New England. From 1785 on, the number and frequency of trading voyages to the region increased steadily. Both Barkley and Gray came as traders, though their explorations proved more important than their commercial missions.

The most effective of all the early explorers of the Pacific Northwest, however, was not a fur trader but an emissary of the British government. Captain George Vancouver arrived in 1792 with two assignments. He was to meet with a Spanish representative to discuss details of a treaty, and "to examine and to survey" the western shore of the continent and chart its inlets and waterways.

Vancouver had seen this coast in 1778 as a midshipman with Cook, and he was eager to return. Although his diplomatic duties ended in stalemate, he accomplished his other objective with distinction. His mapping of the northwest coast over a period of three years brought an end to its long obscurity and rendered a major service to the world's scholars and travelers.

THUS IT WAS SETTLED, at least for half a century, that there was no open, deepwater course to this remote land from the Atlantic except by the long and tedious routes around Cape Horn or the Cape of Good Hope. The alternative was overland: some combination of rivers, lakes, and unblazed trails across the vast wilderness west of the Mississippi.

The newly established government of the United States had had little time to think about that great expanse of backcountry, most of which in any event was claimed by European powers. But then, in 1803, President Jefferson's envoys negotiated the Louisiana Purchase, acquiring from Napoleon an immense tract extending from New Orleans to Montana. To Meriwether Lewis and William Clark the President gave the assignment of investigating the western lands. And in entrusting that responsibility to the two young captains, Jefferson recognized that the logical goal of their exploration was not the somewhat vague limits of "Louisiana" at the edge of the Rocky Mountains, but the limits of the continent at the Pacific Ocean.

With their small Corps of Discovery, Lewis and Clark set out from a point near St. Louis in May 1804 and followed the Missouri River, the Clearwater, Snake, and Columbia, overcoming difficult mountain passages in

*Generous rainfall nurtures the verdant shoreline
of the Pacific Northwest. The annual average ranges
from 60 to 110 inches—not enough to produce dense rain
forests like those farther inland on the Olympic Peninsula,
but still in an abundance that clothes much of the coast
with thick woodlands. Oregon's fertile valleys
give way, north of the Columbia, to Washington's
south-coast bays and beaches, then long stretches
of roadless wilderness in national-park and Indian lands.*

between. After 18 arduous months, in November of 1805, Clark recorded that the party had beheld "with estonishment . . . this emence Ocian."

Within little more than a decade, both by sea and by land, determined men had unlocked the distant and mysterious Pacific Northwest.

TODAY THE REGION'S MAJOR CITIES include three busy seaports, none of which is near the ocean shore. Portland, Oregon's largest city, grew up at the confluence of the Columbia and Willamette rivers, adjacent both to water commerce and to fertile farmlands. Seattle and Tacoma, anchors of Washington's principal metropolitan area, share the great mountain-ringed harbor of Puget Sound. So in both states the urban economic and population pressures are inland. Most of Oregon's coastside towns began as farm communities or modest fishing or lumber harbors; the largest is Coos Bay, with a population of about 14,500. In Washington the oceanside towns are much fewer, and the most populous is Westport, with 1,500 residents. There are larger places with direct access to the sea—Aberdeen, Hoquiam, and Raymond—but they sit on the inland side of large bays.

The climate of western Oregon and Washington is startlingly different from that of most of California, which receives much less rain and almost none of it in the summer. Eureka, California, averages 40 inches a year and only a few tenths of an inch in July or August. Brookings, Oregon, only 85 miles away and five miles beyond the border, gets twice as much rain—80 inches a year, including an average of an inch each summer month.

Oregon's dramatically sculptured coast is one of the world's classic shorelines. Almost all of it is visible from the coast highway or from side roads. Broad vistas from high vantage points alternate with close-up views of spray-washed sea stacks and quiet coves. Back from the water, the green southern Oregon hills grazed by sheep and cattle give way to the famed sand dunes and pine groves of Siuslaw National Forest. Then come the meadows and fields of dairy farms in the northern valleys.

Across the Columbia in Washington, long, flat, sandspit beaches nearly enclose Willapa Bay and Grays Harbor. North of Moclips, the remaining shoreline is one of the least known and least accessible in America. More than half of it is the seacoast section of Olympic National Park; most of the rest is Indian land. Over this last hundred miles, the population density of a coastal strip five miles wide is less than eight persons per square mile. It is, one might say, a long way from Santa Monica.

"The perfect place for an artist"

SOMEHOW I MISSED the big state-line highway sign as I drove north from Smith River, California. On the Oregon side the seaside farms looked just the same, and I was on the outskirts of Brookings before I realized I had crossed the border.

But I had left the towering red-woods behind and that, it was soon apparent, was one lasting difference. The stage that had been dominated by those majestic trees was now given over to seascapes of startling grandeur.

Like northern California, coastal Oregon is essentially rural. Portland, though a major seaport, is 50 miles from the Pacific by air and nearly a hundred by the Columbia River. The state's other principal population centers are scattered up the Willamette Valley. Only a few roads climb the Coast Range to link the interior with the ocean—and not a single one for the first hundred miles, from the border to Bandon.

In addition to being free of large cities, the Oregon coast is open to the public for recreational use. Many far-sighted officials and public-spirited citizens helped bring this about, but the main credit goes to two men: Governor Oswald West, who in 1913 persuaded the Legislature to declare the beaches public highways, and Samuel H. Board-man, who as first superintendent of state parks from 1929 to 1950 carried out a major site-acquisition program.

Today 90 state parks and waysides dot the coast, augmented by federal, county, and municipal lands; and elsewhere state law provides for easements for access to the shore. Of Oregon's 362 miles of seacoast, most can easily be reached and enjoyed by the public. It is not at all surprising that this coast has been called "the most beautiful and most wisely developed stretch of shoreline in America."

Tree-shaded Brookings, both a fishing port and a retirement town, welcomes its visitors with flowers—daffodils that brighten winter days, azaleas broadcasting their color and fragrance from April to June, lily fields in bloom in July, home gardens carefully tended through summer and fall.

For the northbound traveler, Brookings and its rock-studded oceanfront mark the threshold of one of Oregon's most spectacular stretches of highway, some 55 miles of U. S. 101 to Port Orford. Much of it, especially at first, runs along the flanks of steep slopes that in some places rise to heights of 2,000 feet. Heavy rainstorms periodically cause landslides here, and highway engineers routinely reshape the road where slices of mountain have fallen away. For 11 miles the *(Continued on page 167)*

(Continued on page 167)

Durable as the fine wood he shapes, Edsil Hodge stands ready with a pickaroon to pull cut lumber from the mill behind him. He works at the House of Myrtlewood in Coos Bay. There craftsmen fashion a wide range of objects—goblets and coffee mills, owls and elephants—from close-grained Oregon myrtle, known farther south as California laurel.

At Pistol River, Lisa Ward eats a snack outside the general store. High-school boys cool off by splashing into nearby Deep Creek swimming hole. To the north, near Bandon, Charles Panter churns up his flooded bogs with a water reel, dislodging cranberries from the vines so they will float, ready for harvesting. The Bandon area produces 97 percent of Oregon's cranberries—processed, promoted, and distributed by a grower-owned cooperative, Ocean Spray.

Dusk deepens to the hue of sea stacks in Samuel H. Boardman State Park, named for the

superintendent who worked from 1929 to 1950 to keep Oregon's coastline pristine.

Rising with winter mist, smoke from the Georgia-Pacific power plant drifts over Isthmus Slough at the upper end of Coos Bay, one of the world's largest ports for forest-products distribution. At right, logs float in a storage area. At upper right, a boom man whirls his Log Bronc—a boat with a bow-mounted outboard set on a turntable for 360-degree maneuverability—as he sorts logs and steers them onto the inclined lift behind him. A lathe at the top of the lift peels barked logs into thin sheets; dried, glued, and pressed together at high temperature, the sheets become plywood. Formerly the industry burned its surplus by-product wood chips. But now the lumber firms conduct a multimillion-dollar business in the export of wood chips to Japan for pulp.

coastline is within Samuel H. Boardman State Park, an extravagance of jutting headlands, secluded beaches, sturdy sea stacks, and crashing surf.

At the park's Arch Rock Point, I walked through a grove scented by pines and towering Sitka spruce to look out on a congregation of big, rugged rocks just offshore. One, worn through by the sea, gave the spot its name. To the south, the cliffs along the mainland sparkled with slender waterfalls. But the final touch was the most memorable of all. Here and there beneath the trees grew wild iris, both white and lavender, as delicate as any tropical orchid.

A few minutes later, on impulse, I turned onto a road that led among sheep grazing the precipitous hillsides above the highway. In low gear I drove up and up, tires crunching gravel and treads sometimes slipping, until I came to a locked gate almost at the ridgeline. The view from that lofty place held me for long moments: deep green folds of mountain and forest slanting away under a brilliant blue sky to the white-capped Pacific far below.

THE HIGHWAY DESCENDS to sea level near Pistol River, then climbs over Cape Sebastian before reaching the small but lively town—1,750 souls—of Gold Beach. Located at the mouth of the Rogue River, Gold Beach took its name from the metal prospectors panned from the coarse sand of its broad, dark strand. Old-timers still find a few flecks now and again, but Gold Beach's major industries now are timber and tourism, including sportfishing. The Rogue is one of the West's most productive salmon and steelhead streams, and anglers often have their catch custom-canned. To watch the process, I went to Jerry Hull's Rogue River Cannery. Once there, I learned that canning for sportsmen is only a small part of his operation. The plant's main products are commercially canned Dungeness crab, coho (or silver) and Chinook (or king) salmon, and frozen shrimp. In summer most of the ocean catch comes directly into the Port of Gold Beach. In winter, when it's too rough getting in over the bar of the Rogue, it is trucked from Brookings or Crescent City.

That day the emphasis was on shrimp. Dan Reimer, a blond young man in jeans and rubber boots, explained how the shrimp are handled as we clambered up and down stairways to better vantage points.

Kept heavily iced until the processing begins, the shrimp are steamed, then rid of their shells by a conveyor system that rolls, peels, sloshes, rolls again, vibrates, and blows—until they pass into the packing room where they are inspected, placed in cans, weighed, and vacuum-sealed. Then they are frozen and kept at –20° F.

In contrast to the highly mechanized shrimp operation was the salmon canning I saw an hour later for a successful sportfisherman. Jerry Hull cleaned half a dozen 30-inch, ten-pound coho salmon, cut them in cross sections just the right thickness for the flat tins, then helped Inez Briggs lug the full trays to the canning table. Mrs. Briggs has been doing this sort of thing a long time, and in her hands the pieces of pink meat fit snugly and neatly into each can, ready for the lidding machine.

When she asked if I would like to try it, I readily agreed. To my surprise I found my pieces of fish were much more slippery than hers, the sizes obviously more difficult to fit into the can—and the results not nearly so uniform. Mrs. Briggs was amused. "No, no, not that way," she said. "Put the bone inside, toward the center." She paused as I fumbled awhile, then mercifully brought an end to my career by asking,

---

Skeletal trees, smothered by drifting sand, record the Oregon Dunes' encroachment inland—at a rate of 3 to 4 feet a year. Eroded from the slopes of the Coast Range, washed out to sea and carried back to shore, the sand forms wind-rippled dunes as high as 630 feet. These extend a mile or more inland for 40 miles along the coast.

"Well, how do you like your new job?"

From the lidding machine the cans of salmon went to the cooker, and after they emerged they were neatly labeled with the owner's name.

No sportfisherman, however successful, could be more enthusiastic about southern Oregon than Maurine O'Connor. "This is the perfect place for an artist," the tall, slender brunette told me. "The country is beautiful. The air is clear and clean. I feel healthy, and have so much energy. And the earth provides so much—it's easy here to fish and garden—and the people are amazingly generous."

Maurine came to Gold Beach by a roundabout route. Born and reared in Massachusetts, educated in Ohio, she came west to study art and photography at the San Francisco Art Institute. "After a while, I grew tired of the whole frenzied scene," she said. In 1972 she came to Oregon to relax and visit friends —and stayed.

She happily compared Gold Beach ("rural and realistic") with the San Francisco Bay area ("chaotic and competitive") and with Massachusetts where she grew up ("I didn't like the stodginess of the East"). For four years she had been a gourmet cook at a fishing lodge, but at the time of my visit was about ready to become a full-time artist. "I've sold everything I've done. I'm part of the economy now, and I can make it," she said. A painter and designer, she has been specializing in batik fabrics and silk-screening and has collaborated with a friend on a 3-by-9-foot tapestry depicting the river channel, bridge, and hills near the mouth of the Rogue.

"I need to get out once in a while," she said. "I go to San Francisco four times a year to sell, and that's just about right. I'm always so glad to get back!"

Although Maurine as an individual has settled congenially into her new community, newcomers as a class present a somewhat perplexing problem for Oregonians. Most really don't want Oregon's population to grow much bigger than it is, but this is difficult to manage when the state is so attractive.

And that brings up something that other Westerners generally acknowledge. Oregonians tend to be rather unorthodox, perhaps both more independent and more community-minded than many other people. The state has a long history of reform legislation and innovative social-political experiments. It is a state without a sales tax. Its 1967 beach bill guaranteed continued public access to the state's ocean beaches. Its 1972 bottle bill was the first in the nation to ban throwaway beer and soft-drink containers, as a step toward solving environmental and energy-conservation problems. It is the only state I know of that has an all-but-official policy against encouragement of new residents. "Come see us, but please don't stay," is the attitude.

Perhaps Oregon's unpretentious and conscientious personality has been gradually developing almost from the beginning. The pioneers "had come as homeseekers," wrote the distinguished regional historian Charles Henry Carey, and they "created a simple but effective local government, without instruction or command from recognized political authority. . . . Conditions of home life were simple, even primitive, but there was a total lack of pretense and artificiality. Wealth there was none, and there were no grades of social classes."

In any event, her friends are glad that Maurine came—but hope not too many others will follow.

CAPE BLANCO Lighthouse, northwest of the small harbor and quiet streets of Port Orford, stands on the westernmost point of Oregon. Nearby is another gem in the long necklace of coastal parks, with a narrow paved road leading from a landscaped campground down to a broad, curving beach.

In May the coastal hills were bright with the yellow bloom of gorse, an evergreen that a century ago was imported by a landowner from his native Ireland. He set out plantings of it to check wind erosion of his property, and the shrub soon spread throughout the region. For the town of Bandon, gorse brings up unfortunate memories. In 1936 a forest fire ignited thick growths of it and destroyed almost the entire town. Rebuilt, Bandon is now the busy trading center for the surrounding district.

The Bandon area is well known as one of the few places on the Pacific Coast suitable for growing cranberries. On their farm south of town, Charles and Idell Panter and their son and daughter-in-law, Terry and Sara, cultivate 18 acres of cranberry bogs.

"Ours aren't natural bogs, though there are a few around here," Charles Panter explained. "But we do have a peatlike soil, ideal for cranberries."

Panter was a fourth-generation rancher, dairying with his father and two brothers on the Coquille River when he started using his tractor to build cranberry bogs for other farmers. "After a while we decided we might as well build one for ourselves," he said. The Panters put in the first bog in 1949, and it started producing five years later. Eventually Charles moved downstream to give his full attention to raising cranberries.

Dressed in a smart pantsuit, Idell could have passed for a suburban clubwoman on her way to a committee meeting. But Charles assured me that she pulls on hip boots and works as hard at raising cranberries as he does. Together they walked me over the property to explain what goes into building and cultivating a cranberry bog. "This was mostly brushland with some swamps and potholes. We had to clear and burn the brush, take off the topsoil, level the subsoil, replace the topsoil, and add four inches of sand on top of that."

Although the Coos County coast averages 60 inches of rain a year, the Panters have an extensive sprinkler system. The ground must be kept moist throughout the growing period, and the sprinklers also combat both summer heat and winter cold. "If you water on a cold night, ice forms on the plants and insulates them from killing temperatures below 32°," Charles said. Deer are a problem, too. "They love cranberries," said Mrs. Panter. "For that matter, so

does Susie." The black Labrador retriever was trotting beside us, all innocence. "When we're harvesting, she crouches at the water's edge and eats them."

Harvesting normally begins the second week of October and runs through the middle of November. First, the bogs are flooded, then the cranberries are stripped loose with a machine called a cranberry reel. They bob to the surface of the water and are moved by long wooden booms to the edge of the bog. There the berries are loaded into 1,000-pound "tote bins" and trucked to the Bandon receiving plant of Ocean Spray Cranberries, Inc.

One of the nation's most successful farm cooperatives, Ocean Spray is owned by 710 growers who account for 80 percent of the cranberries produced in the United States.

A former flight instructor, control tower operator, and schoolteacher named Pam McGinty manages the Bandon plant. "I'm the only woman in that position for Ocean Spray," she said. "I started in the office here about 1961. Five years ago they needed a new manager, and I was offered the job."

The new, 24,000-square-foot plant puts the berries—350,000 pounds a day at the peak of the season—through a mechanized cleaning process before shipment by truck to a freezing and storage plant in Eugene, 130 miles northeast in the Willamette Valley.

Despite the importance of both agriculture and tourism to Oregon's economy, forest products constitute the state's principal industry. Yet I saw few signs of logging until I reached Coos Bay, the first town of any size along my route. The coastal slopes were logged years ago, and brush or second-growth timber has softened most of the scars. Logging trucks use the coast highway—but not on Sundays or certain holidays, when they're barred from Oregon's public roads.

In Coos Bay there can be no doubt about the significance of the industry. Huge lumber mills crowd the waterfront, the smell of fresh, damp sawdust hangs in the air, and cargo ships loaded with logs and wood products ply the bay waters on their way out to sea.

The main timber species here are Douglas fir, Sitka spruce, Port Orford cedar, and western hemlock. Another tree contributing to the region's economy is the Oregon myrtle, a hardwood prized for its beauty when carved into household articles or costume jewelry.

Offsetting some of the drabness of mill town Coos Bay are its surroundings. Attractive residential neighborhoods push up the wooded hills and into nearby valleys. On the ocean shore to the southwest, two state parks claim special distinctions. At both Cape Arago and Shore Acres the shoreline bluffs, instead of repeating the sculptured basalt of most promontories along the coast, display sharply tilted layers of sedimentary rock. And Shore Acres, once the estate of a lumber-wealthy family, is the site of a botanical garden containing plants brought from many parts of the world on returning lumber vessels.

A mile north of the bay begin the famed Oregon Dunes—since 1908 under the management of the U. S. Forest Service, and now designated as the Oregon Dunes National Recreation Area. For the next 40 miles the great shifting sand formations take over the coast and in places reach inland as far as 2 1/2 miles.

In Reedsport, I talked with John Czemerys at the headquarters of the national recreation area. A veteran of ten years' service here, the genial, sandy-haired Forest Service spokesman is a storehouse of information on the area's natural history as well as its legislative and administrative background.

The Oregon Dunes are among the highest and most extensive coastal dunes in the world; some of them rise to elevations of 630 feet. But what I found most fascinating in John's explanation was the fact that the dunes occupy a slowly but constantly changing zone.

"The sand washes down rivers and streams into the ocean, then drifts ashore," he told me. "Then it's pushed inland by the wind. As it builds up in forested sections, it deprives the tree roots of oxygen and eventually kills the trees. In some cases the sand shifts to leave islands of trees, some on heights, others in depressions or bowls.

"The dunes are generally moving inland about 3 to 4 feet a year; but where it's necessary to protect such things as highways or railroad tracks, the sand has been stabilized with various grasses, Scotch broom, and shore pines."

But now a complication has developed. "European beach grass, introduced about 40 years ago to anchor sandy embankments around certain harbors, has spread into the dunes area," said Czemerys. "Where it has become established it has tended to hold the sand in place and to build up a stable foredune, a sand-and-grass barrier that blocks inland movement of sand from the sea and creates a footing for new growth of conifers, shrubs, and other plants. So, in places, new woodland belts are appearing between the ocean and the eastward-creeping dunes."

Since the woodland belts are expanding more rapidly than the dunes are moving, this "overtaking" trend, if not altered, will mean the eventual disappearance of the dunes.

So, I asked, what is the Forest Service going to do about it? Or is the process inevitable? "Well," replied John, "part of our job is to maintain the scenic values of the area. So we're studying means to reverse the process. The major step under consideration is the removal of certain parts of the foredune to allow a fresh invasion of sand. This would recharge the dunes and destroy the encroaching vegetation."

Later, I tramped across the undulating, curiously beautiful wilderness that brings together desert and ocean. There are certain routes to be found that offer firm footing, but the more fascinating—and challenging—exercise is to strike out across the open dunes. It is hard work. As I climbed, my feet sank and slipped backward in the loose, fine sand. Soon my muscles began to ache, my lungs to labor. But once I reached the ridgeline that was my goal, there was ample reward: a sweeping view over a rippling, dazzling expanse that joined with the ocean, forest, and sky in a rare tapestry of blue and green and white. Standing there, looking out, breathing deeply, I thought once again how intricate are the puzzles of ecology—and how delicate their balance.

The Oregon Dunes extend north almost to Florence, nudging U. S. 101 slightly inland. A short distance beyond Gardiner and its sprawling plywood plant and paper mill, the highway plunges into a thick conifer forest. Here the roadside is dense with shrubs, and in May the rhododendrons had unfurled their fragrant blooms in big splashes of pink against the dark green backdrop.

At the entrance to Florence the Siuslaw River drawbridge was rising. As I waited for a passing sailboat, I wondered why so many bridges along Oregon's coastal highway have a distinctive architectural grace, their arches enhanced by bold incised pillars and towers. Later I saw still other examples at Waldport and Newport, and learned that their special flair could indeed be traced to the influence of one man: C. B. McCullough, chief bridge engineer for the Oregon Highway Department from 1919 to 1932, who strongly believed that bridges should be pleasing to the eye as well as soundly built.

As THE DUNES run their course, the coastline regains its rugged character, and soon the highway begins to climb again. A dozen miles north of Florence it widens for the visitors' entrance to Sea Lion Caves, one of the world's largest ocean grottoes, and the only Stellar sea lion rookery on the American mainland.

The spotless white buildings of the privately owned attraction sit high above the sea amid plantings identified by unobtrusive signs. White-flowered thimbleberry and pink-blossomed salal were both in bloom, along with the gorse and rhododendrons. On the cliff below, hundreds of black cormorants nested, and at the water's edge some of the cavern's large colony of sea lions occupied several rocky shelves. I watched a tawny mother teaching her youngster about the surf, employing the sink-or-swim method. As the pup hesitantly approached the edge, an oversize wave suddenly caught him and swept him out of sight. Seemingly unconcerned, the mother turned toward the cliff. Four or five waves later, the pup came skidding back onto the ledge. Shaking his head, his flippers slipping and sliding, he hunched off after his mother. She barely glanced at him.

By elevator I descended 208 feet to the sea-level cavern. From an observation gallery I could look out into an ocean-carved room 125 feet high and covering a good two acres. Dozens of sea lions, undisturbed by the waves smashing through the grotto's entrance, lounged or heaved themselves about. Some dozed as others grunted or roared, adding to the incessant noise of the surf.

Back at the top of the cliff, I had a clear view of the round, white tower of Heceta Head Lighthouse, whose powerful lamp has been blinking every ten seconds since 1894. But it was at Cape Perpetua that I saw one of the most inspiring panoramas on the entire Oregon coast. To the south, ranks of evergreen headlands within the Siuslaw National Forest rise steeply from the sea; to the north, low-lying, grassy capes backed by wooded hills alternate with wave-fringed bays. The afternoon had been dark and threatening; but suddenly the sun broke through, scudding rainclouds gave way to billowing snow-white cumulus and clearing skies, and as I watched, the ocean turned from sullen gray to exuberant blue.

"People don't really retire around here"

OCEAN RANCHING of salmon? I had heard of avocado ranches and chinchilla ranches, but never before a salmon ranch. At the busy charter and commercial fishing town of Newport, I turned toward the bay front to ask some questions about an important venture in aquaculture.

Beyond a sign reading "oreAqua" I walked past new asphalt holding ponds and concrete channels and fish "ladders" with Vern Jackson, the tall young site manager. "This is what we call a release and recapture facility," he told me. "It operates in conjunction with our hatchery at Springfield, in the Willamette Valley. The young fish, called smolts—coho, Chinook, and chum salmon—are trucked from the hatchery, then held here and fed for several weeks while they adjust to the ocean environment. They're also marked for future identification with coded wire tags. Then they're released into Yaquina Bay.

"The cohos will stay at sea about 18 months; the chums and Chinooks average 42 months. Then—if they haven't been eaten by predators or caught by fishermen—their homing instinct brings them back here, right up our ladders, and we collect them."

I asked whether the project was yielding a marketable harvest yet.

"So far, we're using all the returning fish for brood stock," Vern answered. "But eventually we hope to release a total of 80 million smolts a year from here and a proposed second site at Coos Bay. If we get the 1 to 3 percent return we expect, that could mean an annual harvest of as many as two and a half million salmon."

Oregon Aqua-Foods Inc. was started in 1972 soon after commercial salmon ranching was legalized by the Oregon Legislature. In 1975 the Weyerhaeuser Company bought oreAqua and expanded the operation.

"The biggest problem has been acquiring enough eggs," Vern said. "The supply from state and federal hatcheries is limited. That's why our emphasis now is still on brood stock."

Since the large releases planned by oreAqua are expected to replenish the ocean supply of salmon, some commercial fishermen, charter boat operators, and sportfishermen believe they too will be benefited by the new program.

In addition to oreAqua and a large commercial fishing fleet, Newport boasts Oregon State University's Marine Science Center. The town is also the location of another highly regarded institution, Mo's Restaurant. Friendly, informal, furnished with bare wooden tables and benches, it does a thriving business. I had (Continued on page 185)

Amid straw and spiderwebs at the edge of his father's hayloft in northwestern Oregon's Tillamook County, Brian Porter, 11, balances comfortably on sturdy beams. He often plays here, above the Jersey cows he helps to tend. The coast's temperate weather favors agriculture; prosperous farms—especially dairies—fill the river valleys.

Mountains of the Coast Range rise beyond lush pastures in the Nehalem Valley in Tillamook County. Year-round coolness, 80 to 100 inches of annual rainfall, and a growing season of six to seven months produce rich grasses for the cows that make this the leading dairy county in the state. Ron Myers proudly hefts a Holstein calf 12 hours old. Since buying his 180-acre farm in 1964, Ron has developed one of the finest herds in the valley. Good dairymen here start young. Matt Marti hugs the heifer he raised at age 11 and exhibited at the 1977 county fair. He and the Holstein took a red ribbon. Tillamook's prizewinning cows give 200 million pounds—25 million gallons—of milk a year; much of it goes into the area's most famous product: natural cheddar cheese.

"**P**ig 'n' Ford" races enliven the Tillamook County Fair in August. Tense but grinning, "Punk" Dunsworth perfects his grip before the 1977 event. At the starting gun, each contestant grabs a pig weighing 30 to 50 pounds, cranks his stripped-down Model T, and zooms around a half-mile dirt oval. After each circuit he kills his engine, returns his porker to a pen, wrestles a new partner into his arms, and sprints back to the car. During the races, competitors display heroic leaps; the first man to complete three laps in the finals—safely penning up his final passenger—wins the "world championship."

Winter whitens northern Oregon, and placid horses wait it out on a farm a few miles from the Pacific. Beyond a hay rake, Holsteins huddle in a nearby pasture dappled by the same storm. Snow seldom falls along the coast, and the brief flurries do not paint the ground for long. The sea moderates the climate, bringing cool winds in summer and mild air in winter—when most of the annual precipitation falls as rain. Between November and April, nighttime temperatures may drop below freezing. At left, wood chips rimed with frost glimmer in the cold light of early morning.

Sitka spruce and western hemlock soar skyward through morning mist along the northern Oregon shore. Mushrooms, like the six-inch-tall Amanita inaurata at right, thrive on the forest floor. Many Oregonians still share naturalist John Muir's conviction, "Happy the man to whom every tree is a friend." In the first half of the 20th century, fires destroyed dense stands of timber in Oregon's western forests, prompting the state

government to begin a program of
fire protection and reforestation.
With 30 million acres of forestland,
Oregon has led the nation in
lumber production for 40 years.

As sunset kindles the coastline, a black-tailed deer lingers on the tree-lined cliffs of Ecola State Park. Where forests cloak almost half the state, wood touches many lives. In his farmhouse near Tillamook Bay, Carroll Lee Brooks tries a violin he crafted from Osage

orange. Taking up this hobby in 1956, he has created more than 130 fiddles from a variety of woods. "Violins are like people," he says, "in that they all have different voices." Transforming a salvaged redwood log into Smokey Bear, "Wibb" Ward wields a chain saw "to cut off the wood that doesn't look like a bear." He retired after 35 years as a logger, devotes himself to his unusual pastime, and has populated his ten acres south of Tillamook with bears and other carvings.

been told that Mo's served the best clam chowder on the Northwest coast. I cannot claim to be a fully qualified judge, but my vote was unequivocal. I ate two brimming bowls.

Travelers driving north from Newport encounter an enticing succession of scenic attractions and quiet retreats. State parks draw anglers and beachcombers, along with tide-poolers hoping to observe such creatures as brightly colored sea anemones or spiny sea urchins. Beaches near the mouths of streams are famed for their yields of agates and jasper.

At the Devils Punch Bowl the surf surges in and out of a rock-lined cavity through two wave-eroded holes, violently stirring the salty punch and sending up white plumes of spray.

U. S. 101 angles inland at Oretown, but another paved road heads back to the coast and soon becomes Tillamook County's Three Capes Scenic Route, which links Capes Kiwanda, Lookout, and Meares. Fierce winds at Cape Meares have been trying unsuccessfully for decades to blow away the old lighthouse and a stubborn grove of Sitka spruce commanded by a huge-limbed monarch called the Octopus Tree.

To the initiated, Tillamook is a name to make mouths water. The county is the source of excellent cheeses that are in demand throughout the Pacific states.

Several of the dairy farms are in the broad, green valley of the Nehalem River, where that stream escapes the Coast Range and winds toward the Pacific. Though flanked by mountains sometimes whitened by snow, the valley has a climate mild enough for a six- to seven-month growing season. On its lush grasses the black and white Holsteins, the golden Guernseys, and the fawn Jerseys can graze much of the year.

"The grass is really our only advantage here," said Orval Porter as we walked through his huge barn. "The Willamette Valley has better weather; we can't grow grain or alfalfa. But the grass does well. My two hundred acres of pasture not only grazes 150 Jerseys but also gives me all my silage—maybe 1,500 tons—and some hay as well."

Porter came to the Nehalem Valley in 1926, when he was three years old. He and his wife, June, have reared four children here, two boys and two girls. Walter, the older son, now helps Orval run the farm, and Brian, 11, has already completed a series of 4-H projects. In a well-scrubbed, well-equipped "milking parlor," the two men milk about 130 cows every morning and evening.

Orval regularly gets up at 3 a.m. to begin the day's chores. Despite this, he seemed one of the most contented persons I had met in a long time. "We're happy here," he said. "And the farm is doing fine—so long as we keep on top of things. But you've got to be willing to put in the hours and the work."

Most of the milk from this area goes into the cheese made by the Tillamook County Creamery Association at its plant north of the town of Tillamook.

Large windows allow those in the visitors' hall to watch much of the process from only a few feet away. Cheesemaking is relatively simple, but strict adherence to proven methods is important to quality. Manager D. R. (Pete) Sutton put me into a long white coat and let me wander about the plant. In gleaming stainless-steel surroundings, the milk is given its "starter"—a culture of lactic-acid bacteria—then heated to speed coagulation and the separation of curds and whey. After that, it's a matter of drawing off the whey, or liquid, compressing the curds into firm blocks, then wrapping, storing, and aging.

"Tradition and quality are very important to us," Sutton said. "Cheesemaking has been a major industry in this county since the turn of the century. The farmers here were among the first in the

Stretching from the mouth of the Columbia River south to the California line, Oregon's shore lies open to the people. Legislation in 1913 declared the 262 miles of beaches public highway—for years the main route linking many seaside towns.

country to brand their cheese and advertise it that way. 'Tillamook' has been a registered trademark since 1921."

It was in Tillamook County one morning that a lifelong resident said to me, "People don't really retire around here. They just stop going to their regular work and start concentrating on something different. And a lot of them turn out to be remarkably talented." Examples were all around. My wife, Janice, learned about William (Wibb) Ward during a visit to the Tillamook County Pioneer Museum.

North of Pacific City, about a mile from the ocean, Bertha and Wibb Ward have lived on the same wooded ten acres for 40 years. Wibb's gentle manner belies the rugged, dangerous work he did as a high-climbing logger. The Wards keep their property as neat as a park, and it is often visited by school and church groups, especially for picnics.

But what really distinguishes the place is its population of carved, life-size bears: bears from storybooks, bears from folklore, bears from Wibb's imagination. A walk on his place is full of surprises.

His favorite medium is redwood, which sometimes drifts all the way from California and washes ashore nearby. Ward hauls it home in a tractor-drawn trailer and lets it dry near the barn-studio. Then he roughs out his sculpture with a gasoline-powered chain saw, refines it with a smaller electric chain saw, and finally touches it up with hand tools. The result is one more delightful example of a distinctive folk art.

Thirty miles away, on a small farm near Tillamook Bay, resides Carroll Lee Brooks with his wife, Mildred. "Brooks," I had been told, "makes mighty fine violins." As a sometime violinist I arrived, somewhat skeptically, to see what kind of musical instrument an 83-year-old former cattle homesteader from Montana could produce.

His first effort, completed more than 20 years ago and shown to me with some hesitation, was about what one might expect from a practiced whittler.

But the latest violin he showed me —his 136th!—was a startlingly beautiful instrument with a tone as rich as its polished wood grain. In fact, any one of his last hundred or so is a work of art. By seeking out a wide variety of both hardwoods and softwoods, Brooks has created a collection of astonishing variety in color and grain pattern, some subtle, some flamboyant.

Brooks has learned to do a little country fiddling himself, and plays several of the instruments each day. But, although he has given away some of his violins, they are not for sale. "I get my satisfaction out of making, owning, playing, and showing these instruments," he said. "And also in trying with each new one to surpass the others. After all, satisfaction is the greatest price you can get for anything."

He handed me a violin with a golden-brown finish, made of Osage orange wood from Indiana. I drew the bow over the strings; the tone was firm and mellow. The next one I tried, of monkeypod wood from Hawaii, had a much more brilliant tone.

"Violins are like people in that they all have different voices," my host said. "But almost all my instruments have good voices in the hands of good players. Now, that one got third place down at Mesa." Brooks explained that violin makers assemble annually at Mesa, Arizona. Their products are judged both for tone and for beauty and detail of workmanship.

"One year our newsletter reported that someone slipped in a Stradivarius, just to see what would happen."

He chuckled. "It got fifth place."

THE COASTAL ROUTE resumes its spectacular ways at Neahkahnie Mountain, whose seaside face is an almost sheer basaltic cliff. Into this wall the highway has been cut nearly 700 feet above the water. At Cannon Beach, site of an ambitious sand-sculpture contest each July, I detoured for yet another distraction: Ecola State Park, breathtaking in its combination of wooded hills, grassy glens, and wandering trails overlooking a craggy shore.

In late spring and summer, Seaside

has the holiday, amusement park atmosphere to be expected of a beach resort easily reached by highway from metropolitan Portland. A broad promenade tops the town's two-mile-long seawall and overlooks the beach. There, despite the chill water, enough swimmers and surfers congregate to require a lifeguard tower, one of the few on the Oregon coast. In season, the beach is a choice site for digging razor clams; after dark, driftwood bonfires flicker up and down its length.

But Seaside is also a year-round residential town—with its own special footnote in history. Here, after Lewis and Clark reached the Pacific, members of the expedition set up "5 of the largest Kittles" to extract badly needed salt from the seawater.

At the Fort Clatsop National Memorial a few miles to the northeast stands a reconstruction of the log stockade where the party wintered in 1805-06. It was built in the 1950's through the efforts of the Oregon Historical Society, with craftsmen and business firms donating time and materials.

A swing up to the tip of the peninsula, before I turned eastward to Astoria, took me to Fort Stevens State Historic Park. The old coast artillery post was one of the few places on the continent to draw enemy gunfire during World War II. An exhibit in the visitor center at the park tells this story:

"The post was involved in action by the enemy on the night of June 2, 1942, when [the Japanese submarine I-25] fired nine . . . shells that landed in the vicinity of Battery Russell. . . .

"Later, in September of 1942, the same submarine returned to the Oregon Coast with a different mission. This time the I-25 had on board a small amphibious airplane that was designed to fly a short distance inland and drop fire bombs in the dense forest of southern

Oregon. The small airplane carried out its mission near Brookings but the effort was unsuccessful."

The Japanese tried one other method of harassing the Pacific Northwest: high-altitude balloons carrying both explosive and incendiary bombs. Of some 6,000 balloons launched, a few hundred completed the long journey across the North Pacific. Only two small brush fires were charged to the incendiaries; but one of the antipersonnel bombs took a tragic toll. In May 1945 a Sunday-school teacher on an outing with five children came upon the bomb in the Oregon woods. It exploded, killing all six.

The fatalities prompted officials to reverse a policy of secrecy about the bombs and warn of their presence. Previously, press cooperation with a government concerned about the nation's morale had helped make the random attacks one of the best kept secrets of the war.

And so to Astoria, first permanent American settlement in the Far West. High on Coxcomb Hill rises a remarkable column around which curls a frieze depicting the discovery and exploration of the Columbia River and the founding of the town. An inveterate seeker of good vantage points, I trudged up the 166 steps of the circular stairway inside the column to look out on the confluence of the Lewis and Clark River with the mighty Columbia. Through a steady afternoon rain I could barely make out the broad mouth where the Columbia's currents and the ocean's tides join battle at the formidable Columbia bar. Here are some of the most hazardous waters in the world. In days of fewer navigational aids, the vicinity became notorious as the "Graveyard of the Pacific."

I was to learn more about those waters soon after I crossed the four-mile-long interstate bridge arching out over the channel far below.

"Sunsets, seascapes, dunes and lakes and woods"

AS IF SLAPPED by a furious giant, the big boat recoiled, shuddered, poised a split second, then plunged forward into the trough behind the broken wave. Still upright only because of my safety belt, struggling to get my legs back under me, I leaned forward—and the frigid water that had flooded the protective overhead above the helmsman funneled neatly off a tarpaulin and cascaded down my neck.

"Ready! Get ready! Look out!" came the warning again. And another 14-foot breaker slammed into the boat. Along with Jim Sugar, I was learning something about the infamous Columbia bar, where the powerful river collides with the restless waters of the Pacific. At the U. S. Coast Guard's Motor Lifeboat School at Cape Disappointment, near Ilwaco, Washington, we had joined one of the training crews for an encounter with heavy surf.

"It's a particularly good place—or bad, depending on how you look at it—because there's no consistent pattern; it offers every kind of challenge we need," said Senior Chief Boatswain's Mate Larry Hicks, the school's supervisor. "The Columbia bar is tricky enough under calm conditions. When it's storming, 25-foot breakers are common—and we've seen them as high as 35 feet!"

The vessels used in training are the Coast Guard's 44-foot, self-righting motor lifeboats. Steel-hulled and watertight, with powerful twin diesel engines set deep for a low center of gravity, these amazing boats can muscle their way through the roughest water and, even if capsized, bring themselves right side up within half a minute. Still, they must be maneuvered with great skill if they are to navigate battering seas and rescue someone in trouble.

The day Jim and I went along to watch the students at work was brilliantly clear and windy, with surf running strong and breakers reaching 15 feet. Boatswain's Mate First Class Greg Albrecht was at the wheel; six trainees served as crewmen. As we pulled away from the dock, each of us was wearing a wet suit, life jacket, crash helmet, and a safety belt that could be fastened to some solid part of the boat.

At the end of the north jetty, we turned northwesterly to look for white water. As we moved into heavy swells and the boat began to pitch and roll, we were told to tighten our life jackets and anchor our straps securely. I remember thinking, as we headed into the breakers, "Precautions are fine, but is all this really necessary?" Then, in a chorus of shouts, we hit the first big one, straight on. I never questioned the safety rig again. (Continued on page 201)

Wielding a power saw, a logger near Neah Bay notches a 200-foot Sitka spruce
to control the direction of its fall. A springboard gives the faller good footing above the flaring
base and roots; mosses and lichens reddened by sawdust cover the trunk. Conifers in
several varieties green 80 percent of the Washington coast.

Freighters bound for the open sea (to the right) leave the mouth of the Columbia River between Cape Disappointment in Washington (foreground) and Clatsop Spit in Oregon. Treacherous shoals, strong currents, and mountainous waves at the junction of the Columbia with the Pacific make this some of the most dangerous water in the world. Hundreds of men have lost their lives in the pounding surf. Frequently blanketed by thick weather—fog and raging storms—the river's mouth remained hidden from early explorers of the coast. Ships bypassed the estuary for 200 years; a fur-trading Yankee captain found it in 1792. Thirteen years later, Lewis and Clark followed the lower Columbia to the Pacific, opening the way for eventual commerce along the river. In the 19th century scores of ships heading for Astoria or upriver to Portland came to grief on the estuary sandbars. Now annual dredging maintains a wide shipping channel.

Operation Rescue: Responding to a mock emergency, a helicopter hoists a "victim" from a moving boat on the Columbia; crewmen steady the basket with a tag line (below). This training exercise occurs frequently during winter at the U. S. Coast Guard's Motor Lifeboat School at Cape Disappointment. There, in a three-week course, Coast Guardsmen learn to handle a 16-ton self-bailing, self-righting boat. Designed to survive overturning even in the roughest surf, such boats help save many lives each year. Above, at left, waves breaking over the stern buffet a crewman. Senior Chief Boatswain's Mate Larry Hicks, school supervisor, shouts instructions to a student at the helm.

FOLLOWING PAGES: *Strapped in for safety, helmeted crew members aboard the 44-foot steel-hulled rescue boat "bust a breaker"—a wave running about 12 feet high in the open Pacific just west of the cape.*

Windswept Leadbetter Point, the tip of Long Beach Peninsula, glistens in the February sun. Its marshlands offer food and respite to migratory birds. This wildlife refuge lies at the entrance to Willapa Bay, largest oyster-producing area on the West Coast. Its annual yield: about three million pounds. As low tide exposes an oyster bed, pickers collect the shellfish by hand, working about 20 minutes to fill each slatted tub. Attracting thousands of visitors in summer, the peninsula has a year-round population of some 5,500, including fishermen, artists, and the noted biologist Dr. Vance Tartar. In a one-man lab he calls his shack, he pursues cancer-related research with microsurgery on free-living single cells.

197

Under fog-veiled trees on the Quinault reservation, an Indian checks salmon nets set out along a riverbank. He will sell his catch to an Indian-owned co-op near Taholah. Drawn by the bountiful sea, Indians lived along this shore centuries before white men came to the Northwest. Descendants of these tribes still follow many customs of their seagoing ancestors. During a late-summer festival, Indians race dugout canoes in Neah Bay. These cedar vessels resemble boats used in whaling two thousand years ago. Cooked in true Makah Indian style, salmon secured to cedar sticks bake for an hour over glowing driftwood coals.

The drenching jolt of that wave struck me full in the face and chest, knocked me off my feet, and wrenched a hand loose from one of the two vertical supports I was gripping. Without the belt, I would have been flipped right over the side.

Soon we encountered a series of big waves and pushed our way through them, one after another. I have been whirled around by everything from a pitching horse to a roller coaster to a spinning airplane, but this was the wildest and most exhilarating ride I had ever had. But of course all I had to do was hang on. No responsibility for the boat, no duties, no one to rescue.

The lifeboat school must be one of the American taxpayer's biggest bargains. A conscientious staff of only five petty officers, including Albrecht and Hicks, handles the entire operation.

Staff and students alike freely give major credit for the school's effectiveness to Hicks, a forceful but informal career man who leads by example. But sometimes the pressure and the long hours get to him, and then he declares: "When I retire, my only contact with water will be when it rains."

THE NEAREST TOWN to Cape Disappointment is Ilwaco, a trim little community of pitched-roof houses dating from the early 20th century. Home of one of the largest charter sportfishing fleets in the Pacific Northwest, Ilwaco is the southernmost in a chain of small, water-oriented communities that extends up a slim finger of land popularly called the Long Beach Peninsula. Its western edge is washed by the Pacific, and to the east lie the quiet inlets, the wildlife retreats, and the oyster beds of Willapa Bay.

The largest town is Long Beach, known not only as a seaside resort but also—surprisingly—as the source of what syndicated columnist and gourmet James Beard has called "some of the best chocolate candy in the world." From an old-fashioned kitchen on the main street (I could watch the hand-dipping process through a sidewalk window), the Milton York Candy Company sends its products to mail-order customers all over the country.

The firm's history traces a clear line back to 1877, when a young candymaker named York started selling from door to door in Portland. The present owner, Maxine Levy, and her chief candymaker, Bob Fromhart, use the same copper pots and the same recipes developed by Milton York a century ago.

After a visit to the peninsula in 1977, Beard, a Portland native, wrote: "On the coast of Washington . . . there's an old summer resort town called Long Beach, very quiet and charming, where I rediscovered one of the great candymakers of my childhood . . . . To find something as traditionally good as the York Candy Company still going brings joy to my soul. . . ."

When I tasted some Milton York chocolates, I decided that Beard had not been unduly swayed by nostalgia. Besides, there is the matter of nutrition as well as taste. One of my youngsters has maintained for years that, for mental and physical health, there is a minimum daily requirement of chocolate as well as of vitamins. I kept this in mind as I placed my order.

Chocolate aside, perhaps the most remarkable aspect of this long, slender peninsula is its ocean beach, a broad, flat strand that runs for 28 miles from North Head to Leadbetter Point. Most of the length can be driven in a car—but only on the damp, packed surface between the water and the high-tide line, and there are numerous rules and some obvious risks involved. Tow trucks, in fact, are often seen along the beach.

Tidal streams from the nearby Strait of Juan de Fuca swirl past Tatoosh Island, where a light station keeps automated guard. Sea stacks and forested cliffs check the white surge at Cape Flattery, named by Captain James Cook in 1778. The cape stands nearly 1,300 miles from the Mexican border—at journey's end on the Sunset Coast.

Cold water and strong currents are the rule here, and visitors are warned against swimming and surfing. But there are other pleasures of the shoreline—especially hiking and jogging, surf fishing, stalking the razor clam in season, and beachcombing. Collectors particularly covet the fishing-net floats that sometimes wash ashore after bobbing about for years on their journey from Japanese waters. Some of these colorful glass globes are larger than basketballs.

In the days I spent on the peninsula the name of Larry T. Maxim kept coming up in conversation, and I finally went looking for him. Simply described, he is a professional photographer, but he is far more than that to his fellow citizens. He is considered one of the peninsula's outstanding artists, its most loyal booster, surely one of its most colorful characters. His strong opinions and passionate enthusiasms are forever spilling over.

Wiry and energetic, Larry is as likely to be found plumbing or sawing as standing behind a camera. He will do anything for someone he likes—"and nothing for the other kind." He will refuse, for example, to sell one of his splendid scenic photographs—of which he makes only a single copy, pressed into canvas and custom-framed—if he happens to take a dislike to the potential purchaser.

Maxim and his wife, Stella—whom he calls "MacDuff" for reasons only he knows—discovered the peninsula 11 years ago and, since then, have never wanted to live anywhere else. "It's really a unique place," he said. "Sunsets, seascapes, dunes and lakes and woods. There is indescribable beauty here—but sometimes you have to seek it out, and you have to be receptive. Of course, it's best after the summer crowds leave."

The peninsula's permanent residents number about 5,500, more than 20 percent of them retired. In summer, the population quadruples.

"We're called the north-enders, but actually the whole peninsula is one community," Larry said. "It's all pretty rural, of course. Ilwaco and Long Beach are the only incorporated towns."

Unlike some, Larry Maxim doesn't worry about runaway growth: "Until the Astoria bridge was finished in 1967, it was pretty isolated here, and much of the peninsula was inaccessible even to the residents. The new development we've had so far, with its new roads, has actually opened up more beauty. And I don't think we can really get overcrowded, because the high ground is interspersed with so many marshy places where you can't build anything."

On the opposite side of the peninsula from the Maxims' home at Ocean Park, I visited the Nahcotta waterfront on Willapa Bay, most important oyster-producing center on the West Coast. My first stop was in the office of Vance Lipovsky, a tall young Ph.D. in marine biology. Vance, who has a delightful, high-pitched laugh, is general manager of the Coast Oyster Company's hatchery. Originally from Ohio, he is well content with the peninsula except for its wet climate. "It's no good here if you don't like yourself," he said, "because the rain keeps you cooped up indoors almost all the time."

Much of the hatchery's effort goes into growing special algae as food for the oyster larvae. "This is essentially a farming operation," Vance explained as we walked through the second story of the rambling building. "The cycle starts here." He pointed to some small glass flasks. "Every day we fill 16 of these with sterile water, and add another drop of water containing four million algae cells. The algae multiply by dividing. Eventually, after transfer to larger containers, they go into 500-gallon tanks. At the end of 15 days they are ready to be fed to the oyster larvae."

Downstairs, a different cycle is repeated. "Our objective is to get a continuing supply of eggs for hatching," Vance said. "In nature, the oysters in Willapa Bay usually spawn only in August. So we want to make them think it's summertime. We bring adult oysters from the bay and put them into filtered water at 80° F. for four weeks, then raise the temperature to 90. This causes the male to spawn, and when the female senses this she releases her eggs.

"Then we collect the fertilized eggs—each one barely visible to the human eye—and put them into the big tanks where, as soon as the larvae hatch out, they can begin to feed on the algae. Each of these tanks ends up with more than 100 million baby oysters. With eight tanks, we have close to a billion oysters here at any one time!"

In the big tank, the larva swims about for 15 to 20 days, then permanently attaches itself to a solid object. "The most natural surface is old oyster shell," Vance said, "so we put a supply in the tanks. Here. . . ." He showed me a piece of shell with several small black dots. "These are seed oysters."

After gradual acclimatization in an outdoor nursery area, the seed oysters go into the upper bay, where they grow to maturity in about four years.

Next door, at Wiegardt Brothers, lean, lanky Dobby Wiegardt showed me the fate of the adult oysters. The Wiegardts use natural seed rather than hatchery-grown, getting some from other areas of Washington and some from Japan. But, like Vance Lipovsky's company, they use growing grounds in Willapa Bay. "More than half of Washington's oysters are produced here," Dobby said. "It's one of the cleanest bays anywhere, with no industrial pollution." I watched a line of men and women attacking big, rough hunks of oysters, encrusted and grown together. Their knives skillfully found the crevices and pried open the shells to scoop out the fresh oysters. A conveyor system carried away the empty shells.

We continued through the packing and cold-storage rooms. "A year ago we shifted from canned oysters to fresh raw oysters," Dobby said. "We put them up in ten-ounce jars and ship them by refrigerated truck, mostly to California."

By coincidence, the small population of the upper peninsula includes two doctors of biology with the given name Vance. At the end of my morning with Dobby Wiegardt and Vance Lipovsky, I drove toward Victorian Oysterville, once the lively seat of Pacific County but now a residential hamlet with a historic church and a general store. In the woods southwest of the town, a distinguished scholar quietly carries on one of the many campaigns in the war against cancer. He is Vance Tartar, an Oregon-born scientist whose laboratory is a crude frame structure he calls his shack.

Here is a classic example of basic research in its most unpretentious form. Dr. Tartar's principal interest is single-cell organisms. "I decided that the research I wanted to do, I could do by myself," he said. "It mostly involves microsurgery on living cells, a matter of manual skill, not big machines. All I needed was a good microscope."

A Yale graduate who taught at several major universities, Dr. Tartar was working in the East when he decided to make his home in Washington. In 1948 he came to the Long Beach Peninsula, where he met his wife, Emogean.

"I find big institutions very distracting, and I always wanted to be independent," he said. "I once worked in a seven-million-dollar laboratory, and its endless halls looked just like Sing Sing prison. I couldn't see a tree or a blade of grass. Here sometimes I look out the window and see a black bear running across the meadow."

From his study we walked down a slope to the snug laboratory where he has done work that has gained him an international reputation. Grafting cells together, altering cells surgically, observing the results, Vance Tartar has found what may prove important clues to the reasons for the cellular malfunction called cancer.

"I fell in love with nature as a boy," he said. "That's how I got into all this in the first place. And living here in the woods contributes to my work. It's a fascinating challenge to try to get to the heart of the matter. Discovery! Discovery is the whole thing!"

Nature has taken two big bites out of the southern Washington coast at Willapa Bay and Grays Harbor. The distance from Leadbetter Point, at the northern tip of Long Beach Peninsula, to Cape Shoalwater on the opposite side of the entrance to Willapa Bay is only about four miles. But there is no ferry; and by road around the bay and across the Willapa River bridge at Raymond, the distance is almost 90 miles. Understandably there is not much contact between the peninsula and the towns to the north.

From Cape Shoalwater the resorts and beaches continue to Westport, whose bayside marina is home port for a large commercial and sport charter fleet that fishes the rich salmon grounds nearby. ("At 6:30 . . . the sky was clear—a wonderful event along Washington's green-green coast—and there was no wind," wrote one enthusiast about a Westport fishing expedition. "I knew in my heart that the ocean was full of salmon.") Westport is also the base for the Grays Harbor pilots who guide seagoing ships across the bar and through the bay to Hoquiam and Aberdeen.

In summer a passenger ferry links Westport with the new retirement and resort town of Ocean Shores, on whose southern sands lie the remains of the old coastal steamer *Catala*, wrecked by a storm while at anchor here in 1963. With its long line of beachfront hotels, Ocean Shores hopes to become a major convention center.

Other communities well known to razor-clam enthusiasts reach on northward, their flat, dark beaches alternating with low dunes. Beyond Copalis Beach the coast becomes more irregular, with cliffs, wooded promontories, and offshore rocks. The resorts end at Moclips, near the border of the 190,000-acre Quinault Indian Reservation, but the highway runs another nine miles to the Indian community of Taholah, where it dead-ends. From here to Queets there is no public road to the coast.

Almost the entire Quinault reservation was once prime forest land. Today, the tribal council charges in its publication *Portrait of Our Land*, "Resource exploitation practices conducted under the sanction of the BIA [Bureau of Indian Affairs] have nearly liquidated our forest and fisheries resources. . . . The BIA's management of our land and timber can best be termed 'Forestry by Omission.'"

The tribe is party to lawsuits against the BIA and is actively pressing for control of reservation resources under the Indian Self-Determination Act.

After a long inland detour, U.S. 101 swings back to the coast just north of the Quinault town of Queets, and soon enters the Pacific coastal strip of Olympic National Park. From here for almost 60 miles, except for three small Indian reservations—the Hoh, Quileute, and Ozette—the coast is mostly parkland.

For the first 15 miles the highway closely parallels the shore. Campgrounds at Kalaloch beckon, and a lodge and cabins overlook pebbly Kalaloch Creek where it curves out of thick, green forest to join the ocean.

At Ruby Beach, Highway 101 again turns its back on the Pacific, this time for good. From here north, the ocean beaches are for hikers; public roads penetrate to the shore only at the Quileute Indian town of La Push and southwest of Neah Bay near Cape Flattery.

A mile north of Forks, I turned onto the paved road leading toward La Push and the Mora Ranger Station. In summer, La Push is a busy fishing resort, but on this unsettled January afternoon I saw no other car for miles. Sun and clouds vied for control of the sky, there was a brisk breeze, and at La Push the white spray of the surf sparkled whenever the sun came out. Just offshore rose pointed sea stacks and a high, rearing island topped by a fringe of trees.

All was quiet in town and at the Coast Guard pier. Across from the waterfront, two young girls were taking a Sunday-afternoon walk. Blonde Jeanine Penn and Anna Rose Counsell, a pretty, dark Quileute, are both daughters of carpenters, though "here everybody fishes, too." They go by bus to school—sixth grade—in Forks, they said, but they like living in La Push. "It's fun to walk on the beach and explore the tide pools," said Anna Rose. "We like the woods, too, but we have to be careful," added Jeanine. "There are cougars."

Just south of La Push lie roadside parking lots for several beaches reached by forest trails. I walked at first through an airy grove of leafless alders, their bark silvery with lichens, but soon passed into dense woods of second-growth hemlock. Slash from old logging operations was heavily overgrown with vines and ferns as well as younger trees. The wind had died down, and the forest was still; occasionally I could hear the music of a tumbling stream.

Very gradually I became aware of the sound of ocean surf, louder, then softer again as the trail changed course. Then it grew distinct. The trail made a steep descent—and there was a fine wilderness beach with not a soul in sight.

Here again were rocky offshore islands, some in the distance so butte-like in shape that for a moment I conjured the sight of floodwaters filling the high desert at Monument Valley on the Arizona-Utah border.

I T WAS DUSK by the time I had returned to the road and driven to Mora Ranger Station down an avenue of tall, symmetrical hemlocks. The office was dark; but just then the ranger, Ted Sullivan, and park technician Rich Stokes returned from a trail-mending patrol, and soon I was eating a bowl of piping-hot borscht at Beverly Sullivan's dining-room table.

I asked Ted if many people visited the coastal park strip during the winter. "Well, the winters are nothing like the other seasons, of course; but the climate is mild enough that the coastal area gets considerable use year around," he answered. "With the increase in recreational vehicles, we're seeing a lot more winter camping. And there are a good many backpackers, too."

Rich, a Virginian, had been in Washington only three months, but Ted and Beverly are natives of the state. A genial, bespectacled, 29-year veteran of the National Park Service, Ted started work at Olympic before going on to other assignments, "and we're glad to be back. It may seem quiet right now, but things get pretty lively in the summer."

Since the coastal strip contains so much roadless area, and since many visitors have limited wilderness experience, the rangers expect fairly frequent emergencies. "We work closely with the Coast Guard, and their boats and helicopters respond pretty fast," Ted said.

Near the park's northern end lies Cape Alava—site of Ozette Village, one of the most promising archeological finds in North America. Abandoned in the 1930's, the small enclave was inhabited by the Makah Indians for 2,000 years. To reach Ozette you must walk, ride in a boat, or land in a helicopter on the beach. In a car you can get as far as the park ranger station at the north end of Lake Ozette. From there an excellent trail, mostly a boardwalk of red cedar planks raised above the damp forest floor and occasional marshes, winds four miles to the site.

The sound of my boot heels on the cedar echoed through the quiet woods. The misty rain had made the planks slippery, and twice I skidded and fell flat. But mostly as I walked along I thought about the peaceful beauty around me and the special joys of a winter hike: no heat, no mosquitoes or gnats, no snakes.

The route was surprisingly varied: alders and red cedars and Sitka spruce; dense forest and clearings; light woods and thick undergrowth. Here and there stood an unusually tall spruce; one patriarch I judged to be nearly 200 feet.

After 3 1/2 miles the trail dropped down to a rocky beach with massive piles of driftwood. Just above the high-tide line were grassy, shaded campsites. A mile south, ancient petroglyphs embellished Wedding Rock; half a mile north was Cape Alava, westernmost point in the 48 contiguous states, and the site of Washington State University's Ozette archeological excavation.

Dave Huelsbeck, the cordial young field supervisor, and his wife, Barbara Schmieden, showed me around the dig, and then we talked indoors over a warming cup of coffee. The Ozette discoveries have caused great excitement among archeologists, primarily because of the almost perfect preservation of artifacts that record the culture of a community occupied, apparently continuously, from the present century back many hundreds of years. But what has most surprised the site staff is the popular interest in the project. "Despite the four-mile hike, we had more than 20,000 visitors in 1977," Dave said.

"You know, you might think it would get boring way out here, but actually we stay so busy it's hard to get everything done: keeping records, ordering supplies, supervising the dig—in summer we sometimes have up to 60 people working here. Of course, it's much quieter in winter, and there's just a skeleton crew."

Both Dave and Barbara have enjoyed living at this remote location. "We're not really that cut off," Dave said. "We have radio communication with the Park Service, and a Marine helicopter flies in once or twice a month to bring supplies and take out material from the dig. And we usually get away on our days off—hike out and then drive to Forks or Clallam Bay."

Director of the Ozette project is Dr. Richard D. Daugherty of Washington State University. Daugherty first became interested in the site in 1947. Ozette had been occupied by the Makahs until as recently as the 1930's, when the last of its residents—dwindling in number for a generation because Ozette had no school—finally moved to Neah Bay. Daugherty found Ozette "clearly the largest and richest archeological site along the Washington coast." Three primary factors have contributed to Ozette's importance. First, of course, is the long cultural record; second, the fact that the inhabitants enjoyed a wealth of resources, highly developed skills, and a strong artistic tradition; and third, a still unknown number of houses of the village were buried under massive mudflows several hundred years ago. Encasement in thick clay has preserved the houses and their contents. The more than 40,000 artifacts recovered thus far include tools, weapons, household implements, personal items, and art objects—notably a killer whale dorsal fin made of cedar and inlaid with more than 700 otter teeth.

To remove fragile objects from the hard clay, the archeologists at Ozette developed an innovative technique using streams of water: large hoses to wash away the heavy layers, fine sprays to find and remove the artifacts.

Because the investigation is a study of their own ancestors and the site is on Makah Indian land, the Makahs have played a major role in the project, and have nearly completed a large and imaginatively designed museum—officially the Makah Cultural and Research Center—at Neah Bay for study and display of the Ozette collection. Later I toured the spacious center with its red cedar panels and teakwood floors. One exhibit will include a reproduction of a large plank house at Ozette, with an adjacent diorama to show the view out the front door.

The Makah reservation proper, not counting the Makah land at Ozette, occupies 27,000 acres at the northwest tip of the Olympic Peninsula. Neah Bay, a fishing town on the Strait of Juan de Fuca, is the Makah capital, and here the Ozette artifacts are first delivered to a large laboratory where they are carefully classified and, if necessary, stabilized.

"So far we've processed about 35,000 perishable objects," said Gerald H. Grosso, the project conservator. "The simplest procedure is to soak the object in a preservative of 50 percent polyethylene glycol and 50 percent water."

In a warehouse across the way, Jerry showed me a replica of an Ozette whale-hunting canoe that was being painstakingly built, its design and details of workmanship closely paralleling canoe remnants excavated at Ozette.

The Makah nation's cosponsorship of the Ozette archeological project and the related launching of the new museum have been major interests of the tribal council. I met one afternoon with Jerry Lucas to ask about other activities of the council. Articulate, concerned, confident, Lucas at 31 is the youngest of the five councilmen. Like many of his generation, he has lived off the reservation and found he didn't like city life. "I belong here. I'm just more comfortable," he said.

The bitterness I had found earlier among the Quinaults toward the Bureau of Indian Affairs apparently is not shared—at least as deeply—by the Makahs. They and the BIA cooperate in many ways. "We contract with the bureau to provide certain services, such as police and fire protection," Jerry said. "And we're both involved in resources management—our foresters and their foresters work together, for example."

My guide at Neah Bay was Jonni Trettevick, a round, personable, and obviously popular young Makah who works in the forestry division of the Bureau of Indian Affairs. In addition to showing me the museum and the tribal and BIA offices, she either took me to or pointed me toward the medical center of the Indian Health Service, the high school gymnasium with its geometric Indian motif, the bay's fishing piers and log boom, the Coast Guard station, and outlying Makah Air Force Station.

In the late afternoon I drove past the totem pole in the middle of town, past the horses grazing at streetside, and out onto the network of logging roads that crisscross the peninsula between Neah Bay and Cape Flattery. As I climbed, I caught marvelous views out over the Strait of Juan de Fuca to the long, green coastline of Canada's Vancouver Island. Finally I came to a roadside turnaround and two wooden signs nailed high on trees. One warned: "Rugged High Cliffs. Enter at Own Risk." The other said, "Cape Flattery Trail."

Beneath towering conifers I followed the rough, descending trail to its end. I was standing on a rocky slab perhaps 30 feet above the ocean. Ahead, like a final punctuation mark, stood Tatoosh Island, crowned by its lighthouse.

Except for the blinking light and my own intrusion, how timeless it all seemed! These rocks were here when Captain Cook sailed by, and the sounds of the wind in the trees and the surf on the rocks below had lulled some aborigine thousands of years before that.

As sunset neared, streaks of cloud low in the western sky were preparing something worthwhile. Contentedly I settled down to watch.

Now that the months of exploring the Sunset Coast are behind me, perhaps I can sum up my most lasting impressions this way:

This slender ribbon of land and water, as we have called it, is remarkable in many ways—in its beauty, its variety, its climate, its promise. And the people who live along this ribbon recognize that, both because of the nature of the coastline and the nature of the sea, they are sharing in a special experience.

They are *conscious* of the ocean. I have known people who live in the woods yet never focus on a tree trunk or a leaf; people who live in the desert yet never try to understand it; people who live in the city yet never make friends with it. But the people I met who live beside the sea are aware of it, appreciate it, study it, love it, and fear it. They walk beside it at dawn, pause at evening to watch the sun slip beyond its horizon, frequent its piers and rocks to cast in their fishing lines, explore its tidal zones and offshore islets. They refresh themselves by breathing its salty air, swimming in its swells, riding its breakers.

The sea is not a self-effacing partner. It is aggressive and demanding. If it cannot captivate you with its beauty, it will force your attention with its violence. It will tease you, tire you, threaten you; but it will seldom bore you.

All this the people who live here understand, and they respond. And that, more than any other one thing, is what I learned. Life along the seacoast, and specifically along the Sunset Coast, is unlike life anywhere else.

Acknowledgments

The Special Publications Division is grateful to the individuals and organizations named or quoted in the text and to those listed here for their generous cooperation and assistance during the preparation of this book: Gene Abbett, Marge Booker, Leonard J. Brady, Dan Brown, James M. Cardwell, Charles R. Colgan, Arnold Court, Terry DiMattio, Theodore R. Dudley, Clifford H. Fiscus, James G. Fisher, Anne K. Foote, Mr. and Mrs. Donald Fraser, Stanley P. Gessel, Thomas E. Hamilton, Richard L. Kline, Mr. and Mrs. Charles Lane, Charles M. Lawrence, Arthur Lessard, Michael Levitt, George I. Loveland, John W. Massie, Ron Miller, Rosemary Miller, James R. Moriarty III, Gordon B. Oakeshott, Ted Owen, Gerald L. Partain, Rick Pflaum, John B. Pinto, Bernard W. Pipkin, J. J. Poindexter, Sally Reeve, Joseph L. Reid, Richard L. Ridenhour, Steve Robinson, Jim Row, Francis P. Shepard, Mr. and Mrs. Bernard Silbert, Special Equipment Shop of NGS, Kathryn A. Straton, Steven L. Timbrook, Royce Tooker, Stephen D. Veirs, Jr., Paul W. West, Wayne C. Wheeler, Raymond A. Yost, Mr. and Mrs. Jerry Zimmer.

Additional Reading

The reader may want to check the National Geographic Index for related articles, and to refer to the following books: Mary W. Avery, *Washington: A History of the Evergreen State;* Walton Bean, *California: An Interpretive History;* Dennis Brokaw and Wesley Marx, *The Pacific Shore: Meeting Place of Man and Nature;* Charles H. Carey, *General History of Oregon: Through Early Statehood;* John W. Caughey, *California: A Remarkable State's Life History;* Norman H. Clark, *Washington;* Gordon B. Dodds, *Oregon;* Otis W. Freeman and Howard H. Martin, eds., *The Pacific Northwest: An Overall Appreciation;* James A. Gibbs, *Pacific Graveyard;* Amos L. Hood, *Beachcombing the Pacific;* Ruth A. Jackson, *Combing the Coast: San Francisco Through Big Sur;* Don Greame Kelley, *Edge of a Continent: The Pacific Coast from Alaska to Baja;* David W. Lantis, *California: Land of Contrast;* David Lavender, *California: Land of New Beginnings;* Jack McDowell, ed., *Discovering the California Coast;* William L. Mainwaring, *Exploring the Oregon Coast;* Neil Morgan, *The California Syndrome;* Gordon B. Oakeshott, *California's Changing Landscapes: A Guide to the Geology of the State;* Edward F. Ricketts and Jack Calvin, *Between Pacific Tides,* rev. ed. by Joel W. Hedgpeth; Francis P. Shepard and Harold R. Wanless, *Our Changing Coastlines;* Bill Speidel, *The Wet Side of the Mountains.*

Library of Congress CIP Data
Windsor, Merrill, 1924-   America's Sunset Coast.
    Bibliography: p. 208 Includes index.
    1. Pacific States—Description and travel—1951-   2. Pacific States—History—Miscellanea.   3. Pacific Coast (United States and Canada)—Description and travel.   4. Windsor, Merrill, 1924-
    I. Sugar, James A.   II. National Geographic Society, Washington, D. C. Special Publications Division. III. Title.
F852.2.W56   979   77-93401   ISBN 0-87044-253-8

Composition for AMERICA'S SUNSET COAST by National Geographic's Photographic Services, Carl M. Shrader, Chief; Lawrence F. Ludwig, Assistant Chief. Printed and bound by Kingsport Press, Kingsport, Tenn. Color separations by Graphic South, Charlotte, N.C.; National Bickford Graphics, Inc., Providence, R.I.; Progressive Color Corp., Rockville, Md.; The J. Wm. Reed Co., Alexandria, Va.

Long, sharp needles in bundles of five distinguish the rare Torrey pine, which has a natural range limited to sparse groves on Santa Rosa island and the dry mesa of Torrey Pines State Reserve. When exposed to the force of sea winds, these sprawling evergreens grow almost parallel to the ground and become twisted into bizarre shapes. Those protected from the winds stand straight and tall.

BACK ENDPAPER: *A solitary great blue heron stands motionless at the mouth of the Waatch River in far northwestern Washington as sunset streaks the sky.*

Index

Boldface indicates illustrations;
italic refers to picture legends (captions)